RANDOM HOUSE
LARGE PRINT

IF DEMOCRATS HAD ANY BRAINS, THEY'D BE REPUBLICANS

ALSO BY ANN COULTER
AVAILABLE FROM RANDOM
HOUSE LARGE PRINT

Godless

IF DEMOCRATS HAD ANY BRAINS, THEY'D BE REPUBLICANS

ANN COULTER

RANDOM HOUSE
LARGE PRINT

Library of Congress Cataloging-in-Publication Data
Coulter, Ann H.
If Democrats had any brains, they'd be Republicans /
by Ann Coulter.—1st large print ed.
p. cm.
ISBN: 978-0-7393-2738-8
1. Liberalism—United States. 2. United States—
Politics and government—21st century. 3. Large
type books. I. Title.
JC574.2.U6C674 2007b
324.2736—dc22
2007032866

www.randomhouse.com/largeprint

FIRST LARGE PRINT EDITION

10 9 8 7 6 5 4 3 2 1

This Large Print edition published in accord with
the standards of the N.A.V.H.

Jacket design: David Tran
Jacket photograph: © Shonna Valeska

FOR
EFFIE TEN EYCK VAN VARICK

(1718–1782)

CONTENTS

Introduction: Liberals and the Woman
Who Hates Them 1

Airport Security: Make Imams Take Buses 52

Baby-Killing: Abort Liberals, Not Children 60

Blacks: The Only Thing Standing Between the
Democrat Party and Oblivion 66

George W. Bush: The Guy I'd Most Like to Have a
Nonalcoholic Beer With 76

Christians: Must Reproduce More 81

Bill Clinton: He Left a Mark on History That
May Never Come Out 89

Hillary Clinton: The Smartest Woman in
the World! 100

Contents

Colleges: The English Translation of "Madrassa" . 105

Communism: A New Fragrance by Hillary Clinton . . 113

Ann Coulter: My Quotes About Me! 120

Crime and Punishment: Preferably a
Two-Step Process 133

Dear Ann: Free Advice Worth Every Penny 138

Democrat Ideas (See Also: Marx, Lenin) 141

Democrats' Virtues: Points of Light in a
Sea of Darkness 149

Elections: It Only Encourages Them 151

Environmentalism: Adolf Hitler Was the First
Environmentalist 158

Evolution, Alchemy, and Other "Settled"
Scientific Theories 163

Foreigners, or the "Non-Soap-Oriented" 168

Gays: No Gay Left Behind! 172

Girls: Chicks Hate It When You Call Them "Girls" . . 180

Guantánamo: Room Service, I'd Like Seventy-two
Virgins, Please 184

Guns: The Constitutional Right You Can Carry in
Your Purse 189

Contents

Hollywood: They Ought to Be Committed—
Oops, They Already Are! **196**

Immigration: This Is Ours, That Is Yours . . .
Say, Do You Do Windows? **201**

Iraq: A New Reality Show **206**

Teddy Kennedy: Apparently Fat, Drunk, and
Stupid **Is** a Way to Go Through Life **214**

John Kerry: "Who Among Us Does Not
Love NASCAR?" **219**

The Language Police: Can't We Have More
Real Police? **226**

Liberal "Argument": Hissing, Scratching, and
Hair-Pulling **236**

Liberalism and Other Psychological Disorders **245**

"Liberal Patriotism" and Other Oxymorons **255**

Liberal Religion: American Idolatry **265**

Liberals in Alphabetical Order, or Why I
Sometimes Waver on Abortion **276**

Liberal Tactics: Distortion, Dissembling, Deception—
and the Rest Is Just Run-of-the-Mill Treason **287**

McCarthyism: Calling Communists
"Communists" **294**

Contents

The Military—Their Pet Peeve: Keeping George
Clooney Safe 306

Morals: Get Chuck Schumer Over Here, I Don't
Want to Have to Explain This Twice! 315

Muslims: Santa Claus, the Easter Bunny, and a
Moderate Muslim Walk into a Bar 323

The **New York Times:** Don't Look Now, but the
Old Gray Lady Is on a Respirator 332

Old Media: Imagine an Open Sewer with Coupons,
Want Ads, and Your Horoscope 339

Ronald Reagan, or Why I Sometimes Waver on
Human Cloning 353

Republicans: Aren't They Magnificent? 358

Scandals: There's a New Museum Dedicated to
Them in Little Rock, Arkansas 366

Sex: "Virile Pacifist" Is an Oxymoron 375

The Supreme Court: I Haven't Been Officially
Approached as Yet, but Thanks for Asking 379

Taxes: How About Amnesty for "The Wealthy"? . . . 390

The War on Terrorism: Peacenik Pacifists to
the Rescue! 394

Acknowledgments 411

IF DEMOCRATS HAD ANY BRAINS, THEY'D BE REPUBLICANS

THE TRUTH CANNOT BE DELIVERED WITH NOVOCAINE.

—ANN COULTER,
Hannity & Colmes,
6-7-06

INTRODUCTION:
LIBERALS AND THE WOMAN
WHO HATES THEM

Uttering lines that send liberals into parox-
ysms of rage, otherwise known as "citing
facts," is the spice of life. When I see the
hot spittle flying from their mouths and the
veins bulging and pulsing above their eyes,
well, that's when I feel truly alive. This happens, I dearly hope, once a week when my
column is released. But the public gnashing
of teeth that I incite occurs approximately
every six to eight months, which is rather
peculiar, since I believe I annoy liberals
much more often than that.

Liberals' response to unbridled right-wing
speech makes the Muslims look laid back.
Reacting with stupefied indignation when-

ever someone disagrees with them—especially in a way that makes people point and laugh at liberals—they seem to be in a constant state of outrage. Liberals, and the conservatives who fear them, have a look of perpetual outrage, kind of the way Nancy Pelosi has a look of perpetual surprise.

About twice a year for nearly a decade, I have upset the little darlings with some public statement, and yet they manage to summon fresh outrage for each new offense. Each time they think I can't "sink any lower"—I proceed to do so! And by the way, if they're going to keep using the tired formulation "**This time,** she's gone too far!"—can I get an admission that the last sixteen times were, therefore, not "too far"?

I'm almost at the point that I could put together an entire speech containing only lines that make liberals cry. It would be a rather disjointed speech, involving references to Muslims, Katie Couric, Bill Clinton, Max Cleland, Muslims again, Norman Mineta, Justice Stevens, the Jersey Girls, more on the Muslims, Jack Murtha, John Edwards, still more on the Muslims, and Lincoln Chafee—among many others.

To compensate for all the Republicans who go supine at the sound of liberal squalling, I would include a short section in my speech on Strom Thurmond's contributions to America. I'd fire some of Bush's U.S. attorneys. I'd have a few jokes about Abu Ghraib—which I think I'm entitled to. I suffered more just listening to the endless repetition of those Abu Ghraib stories than the actual inmates ever did. Then I would wrap it up by laughingly referring to a liberal in the audience as a "macaca."

Of course, if I start going around making disjointed speeches that make liberals cry, Barack Obama might accuse me of stealing his act.

Liberal hysteria about conservative speech always follows the same pattern; I call it "The Five Stages of Conservative Enlightenment." There are public denunciations, demands for apologies, letter-writing campaigns, attacks on the sources of your income, and calls for censorship. There will be lots of wailing, but no facts refuting the point behind your hysteria-inducing statement. Liberals prefer denouncing people with idioms—**over the top, gone too far,**

crossed the line, beyond the pale—not substance. Whose line? Whose pale? It almost makes you think they don't want to talk about the substance.

But it turns out that Americans often disagree with liberals. And they seem not to like bullies. Or, for that matter, crybabies. Interestingly, these often seem to be the same people. When liberal censors are unable to persuade Americans not to support you and fail at their attempts to cut off your sources of income, they will accuse you of doing what you do "for the money." Every time Larry King interviews a guest denouncing me as a moneygrubbing demagogue, he pockets about $28,000.

For one or another remark, I've been denounced by Senator Hillary Clinton, Senator John Kerry, Senator Tom Daschle, Senator Dick Durbin, Senator Jack Reed, Senator Dianne Feinstein, Senator Frank Lautenberg, more than fifty Democratic House members, and Republicans like Governor George Pataki, as well as a slew of sissy Republican presidential candidates. Oh also, of course John Edwards for a joke about John Edwards.

In the midst of the hysteria over my having "gone too far," it will be announced that the target of my cruel joke has emerged triumphant, whereas I have finally been vanquished. And then you will never hear from my human punch line again, but I will return to utter another allegedly career-ending statement another day. Don't believe me? Okay, how many times have you seen me on TV this week? How many times have you seen Max Cleland or Kristen Breitweiser on TV this week? I rest my case.

As if it's never been done before, conservatives will be produced to denounce me. In 1998, I wrote **High Crimes and Misdemeanors,** the first of my five **New York Times** bestsellers. **National Review** promptly gave it a rotten review, prissily recommending that Clinton critics like me would "do well to examine their own sense of public decency." Yes, someone actually cited "public decency" to criticize a critic of Bill Clinton. I'll just pop out for a sandwich while those of you blessed with the gift of irony ponder that for a few minutes. I personally preferred the liberal **Economist** magazine's review, saying **High Crimes**

and Misdemeanors "reads like the closing argument of a long trial by a prosecutor who plainly hates the guilty bastard at the defence table."

I have been attacked steadily by some conservatives, generally known as "my competitors," ever since. So the novelty of being attacked by a conservative is beginning to wear off.

The novelty of elected Democrat officials claiming to investigate me has also worn off. Soon after **High Crimes** was published, I received fake subpoenas from Democratic congressmen, demanding information for the impeachment hearings.

On November 16, 1998, Representative John Conyers Jr. (D-Mich.), ranking minority member on the House Judiciary Committee, sent me an official, subpoena-like letter on committee letterhead, demanding all my correspondence or communications with various of my friends for the prior four years, including George Conway, Jim Moody, and Lucianne Goldberg. Conyers is now the chairman of the House Judiciary Committee, which should help you sleep well tonight. He

is violently opposed to listening to the conversations of terrorists, but believes the government should be able to demand copies of
Ann Coulter's birthday cards. Scratch a "civil
libertarian," find a fascist.

I wrote back:

> *Thank you for your correspondence. I
> wish you the best success in your im-
> peachment inquiry.*
>
> *Please correct me if I'm wrong, but
> my understanding is that your committee
> is looking into impeachment of the presi-
> dent. I do not believe you have authority
> to impeach a private citizen for express-
> ing her First Amendment rights by writ-
> ing a book critical of the president. For
> that reason, I have no intention of com-
> plying with your burdensome, irrelevant
> and harassing request that I produce,
> inter alia, phone records, e-mails and
> birthday cards exchanged with several
> of my friends and acquaintances since
> 1994.*
>
> *If it's any help, however, I believe
> that you should be able to obtain the*

same information from Terry Lenzner or another of the president's private investigators.

Love, Ann.

We got the president safely impeached, though sadly not removed from office. I had written a bestselling book to help move that process along, but I was still waiting—and continue waiting to this day—for my check from Richard Mellon Scaife so that newspaper columnists like Gene Lyons who called me a "Scaife-funded blonde" wouldn't be liars.

Before the publication of my second book—and number one **New York Times** bestseller—in June 2002, it was widely proclaimed that my career was over. Finished. Kaput.

"DOES THIS MEAN THE END OF ANN COULTER?" —Alex Kuczynski, *New York Times,* November 8, 1999

"ANN COULTER SEEMS TO HAVE FALLEN BY THE WAYSIDE, NO LONGER ENTICING VIEWERS WITH THE *BASIC INSTINCT* RIDE OF HER MINISKIRTS AND *FATAL ATTRACTION* STARE." —James Wolcott, *Vanity Fair,* February 2001

And with every statement that brought my career to a crashing halt, I continued to write bestsellers. (Thank you, readers!) My career has been "finished" so many times, I've practically made a career out of ending my career. I don't know how else to get this message across to right-wingers: Liberals aren't that scary anymore! Please stop apologizing. The current generation of Republicans seems to be stuck in 1973, living in abject terror of a cruel swipe from the moribund mainstream media and hoping to win recognition as a "thoughtful" conservative. If Adolf Hitler were discovered alive and well and living in the Amazon somewhere, a Republican consultant would advise him to denounce me. Liberals would say, "Okay, he's not so bad. Sure, he's responsible for the deaths of millions of people, but he's right about Ann Coulter." The mainstream media would try to help him—maybe portray him as a victim. Except that no one's watching their TV shows anymore.

Perhaps there are Young Republicans who can learn. So let me stress this point: You don't want to be a member of their club. We are in a tooth-and-claw battle for our nation. This is no time to parse, nuance, or clarify words. Liberals don't rely on words. They judge us on a jurisprudence of epithets. Fight fire with fire. Just call them traitors and let them sort it out.

Here's a short précis of my career-ending statements and the accompanying obituaries—or as I call them, "my finest hours." This isn't a full compilation, since I couldn't remember even half of them. As with most liberal prattle, they're eminently forgettable—as forgettable as Judith Nathan Giuliani's first husband. A few of my obituaries have been especially difficult to track down because they were published in newspapers that are now defunct or written by "journalists" currently selling **Star Trek** memorabilia on the Internet.

These are only the blubberfests where some journalist helpfully used one of the mind-numbing clichés like "This time, she's gone too far," allowing me to find them with ease on Nexis. Many of my alleged career-enders are now memorialized in T-shirts for right-wingers, such as the first quote below. Ozzy Osbourne has his bats, and I have that darn "convert them to Christianity" line. If you have a problem with that, please e-mail me at ann@killtheirleadersandconvertthem tochristianity.com. Some may not like what I said, but it's been six years and I'm still waiting to hear a better suggestion.

SEPTEMBER 2001
"We Should Invade Their Countries, Kill Their Leaders, and Convert Them to Christianity."

WE know who the homicidal maniacs are. They are the ones cheering and dancing right now.

We should invade their countries, kill their leaders, and convert them to Christianity. We weren't punctilious about locating and punishing only Hitler and his top officers. We carpet-bombed German cities; we killed civilians. That's war. And this is war.
— "This Is War," 9-12-01

Our country had just been hit by the greatest terrorist attack in the history of the world. Naturally, liberals immediately turned to the most important business at hand: making sure Ann Coulter didn't hurt terrorists' feelings with harsh language. In liberals' defense, I could have proposed converting the little darlings to anything but Christianity—cannibalism, Communism, scrapbooking—and liberals would not have been so testy.

"EVEN BY HER USUAL INCENDIARY STANDARDS, ANN COULTER'S RESPONSE TO THE TERRORIST ATTACKS WAS SOMETHING OF A JAW-DROPPER." —Howard Kurtz, *Washington Post,* October 2, 2001

"ON SEPTEMBER 13, 2001, COLUMNIST ANN COULTER OFFERED UP THE SINGLE MOST INFAMOUS FOREIGN POLICY SUGGESTION INSPIRED BY 9/11." —Sara Rimensnyder, *Reason,* October 1, 2002

"COULTER PROVED THAT EVEN WHEN AMERICAN BLOOD IS BOILING AND MUCH OF THE MEDIA ARE RALLYING 'ROUND THE FLAG, YOU CAN GO LIGHT YEARS BEYOND THE BOUNDS OF RATIONAL THOUGHT." —Mark Jurkowitz, *Boston Globe,* October 31, 2001

And my personal favorite, praising liberals for not "taking the bait" of a terrorist attack to criticize the terrorists:

"AFTER THE SEPTEMBER 11 ATTACK
MASTERMINDED BY A TERRORIST HOPING
TO SPARK A RELIGIOUS WAR, VIRTUALLY
EVERY OFFICIAL AND PUNDIT KNEW BETTER
THAN TO TAKE THE BAIT. EXCEPT FOR
CONSERVATIVE COMMENTATOR ANN
COULTER. . . . COULTER IS SPINNING HER
DOWNFALL. . . ." —Anonymous Brave Liberal,
Washington Monthly, November 1, 2001

FEBRUARY 2002
On Norman Mineta, Secretary of Transportation

As we enter our seventh year of being forced to undergo body-cavity searches in order to fly commercial airlines in America, please remember, I did my best to get airport security to look for terrorists, rather than treating all Americans as if they are terrorists.

ACCORDING to initial buoyant reports in early February, enraged travelers rose up in a savage attack on the secretary of transportation. Hope was dashed when later reports indicated that the irritated travelers were actually rival warlords, the airport was the Kabul Airport, and Norman Mineta was still with us. . . .

Ethnic profiling is the only reasonable security measure that has been thwarted in the war on terrorism. Every other anti-American, left-wing attack on the war has failed miserably. Liberals denounced military tribunals, FBI interviews with Arab student visitors, the detention of terrorism suspects, monitoring conversations of jailed terrorists, and the treatment of prisoners in Guantánamo.

All to no avail—except ethnic profiling.

The whole country knows that goosing little old ladies boarding planes is not going to make us any safer. . . .

[Mineta] has taken the occasion of the most devastating attack on U.S. soil to drone on about how his baseball bat was taken from him as a child headed to one of Franklin Roosevelt's Japanese internment camps.

As Mineta has endlessly recounted in interviews of late, "I remember on the 29th of May, 1942"—note that he remembers the day—"when we boarded the train in San Jose under armed guard, the military guard, I was in my Cub Scout uniform carrying a baseball, baseball glove and a baseball bat. And as I boarded the train, the MPs confiscated the bat on the basis it could be used as a lethal weapon."

Good God! A guard took Mineta's baseball bat as a child, and as a result he's subjecting all of America to the Bataan Death March! Someone please give him a baseball bat.
— "Mineta's Bataan Death March," 2-2-02

One curious fact about the ensuing outrage is that Hollywood liberals denounced me faster than the Arabs did. Maybe I'm winning the camel jockeys over! After all, they get Christmas presents under my plan.

" 'ANN COULTER'S RECENT ATTACK ON NORMAN MINETA IS DESPICABLE,' SAID PEOPLE FOR THE AMERICAN WAY FOUNDA- TION PRESIDENT RALPH G. NEAS. 'IT IS OUTRAGEOUS TO SAY THAT THIS LONG-TIME PUBLIC SERVANT HATES AMERICA. BUT IT IS UNFORTUNATELY NOT SURPRISING, GIVEN COULTER'S HISTORY OF SIMILARLY RABID COMMENTARY.' " —Statement, People For the American Way Foundation, March 1, 2002

"ADC CONDEMNS RACIST ATTACK ON SECRETARY MINETA, URGES UNIVERSAL PRESS SYNDICATE TO DROP COULTER COLUMN . . . ON MARCH 5, ADC CONDEMNED A RECENT COLUMN BY RIGHT-WING COMMENTATOR ANN COULTER . . . COULTER EXPRESSED REGRET THAT THE AFGHAN TRANSPORTATION MINISTER WAS RECENTLY KILLED INSTEAD OF SECRETARY MINETA." —*ADC Times,* March 5, 2002

Nearly a month after that, more than fifty House Democrats signed a letter asking President Bush to condemn my column: "Ms. Coulter's bigoted remarks can only divide our country during this trying time in our nation's history." Amazingly, this was not preceded by a nonbinding resolution denouncing the First Amendment. Today, of course, Democrats in Congress are claiming they didn't vote to condemn me, they voted to give the president the **authority** to condemn me, so they're not responsible for the mess that followed.

JUNE 2002
The Publication of My Number One *New York Times* Bestseller *Slander: Liberal Lies About the American Right*

"COLUMNIST ANN COULTER HAS REACHED NEW LEVELS OF FEROCITY IN HER LATEST BOOK, *SLANDER.*" —Tucker Carlson, *Crossfire,* June 27, 2002

"[S]HE HAS PRODUCED A PIECE OF POLITICAL HACKWORK. THE DEEPER INTO HER SUBJECT

SHE GETS, THE MORE SHE RESORTS TO THE TOOLS OF CALUMNY AND PROPAGANDA SHE PROFESSES TO CRITIQUE." —Christopher Caldwell, *Washington Post*, July 7, 2002

"THE ANN COULTER QUESTION: HOW TO RESPOND TO A HALF-WIT?" —*San Jose Mercury News*, August 16, 2002

"WHO THE HELL BOUGHT THIS BOOK? COULTER, AFTER ALL, IS PLAINLY ONE OF THE MOST INTENTIONALLY INFURIATING COMMENTATORS AT WORK TODAY. . . . INDEED, COULTER IS SUCH AN INVETERATE NEST FOULER THAT SHE HAS EVEN MANAGED TO ALIENATE PARTS OF HER RIGHT-WING CONSTITUENCY." —Sara Rimensnyder, *Reason*, October 1, 2002

"*SLANDER:* IT JUST ISN'T TO BE TAKEN SERIOUSLY." —Martin Gottlieb, *Dayton Daily News*, August 16, 2002

"[T]HE SMUGNESS AND CONSPICUOUS LACK OF EXPERIENCE AND SEASONING IN THESE TELEBIMBOS [LIKE COULTER] SHOULD GIVE CONSERVATIVES PAUSE. . . . ARGUING WITH THEM IS LIKE PAYING ATTENTION TO

DISOBEDIENT CHILDREN. THEY SHOULD BE TREATED LIKE SPOILED BRATS WHO MOUTH OFF. PUT THEM OVER THE KNEE, PADDLE THEIR FANNIES, TELL THEM TO WIPE THAT SMIRK OFF THEIR FACE AND TO SPEAK UP ONLY WHEN THEY'VE LEARNED SOMETHING ABOUT THE WORLD." —Charles Taylor, Salon, June 27, 2002

Again, I'll save my personal favorite for last. This one was published after **Slander** had been the number one **New York Times** bestseller for weeks, but writer Sara Fritz (whose byline no longer appears in Nexis) was finally getting around to declaring my career over. Liberals are a little slower in Florida. (See my elaboration on this point below.)

"SOME SAY THE HEYDAY OF COULTER-STYLE WOMEN PUNDITS PASSED WITH THE END OF THE CLINTON PRESIDENCY." —Sara Fritz, *St. Petersburg Times* (Florida), July 1, 2002

JUNE 2002
On Katie Couric, the "Affable Eva Braun of Morning TV"

IN a 1999 public appearance, **Today** show host Katie Couric attributed the vicious slaying of gay student Matthew Shepard in Wyoming and of James Byrd, Jr., a black man, in Texas to a climate created by "religious zealots or Christian conservatives." The affable Eva Braun of morning TV authoritatively informed President George Bush (41) that the Republican National Convention had "relinquished too much time to what some term the radical religious right."
—*Slander*

"NOW KATIE COURIC, YOU KNOW MAY BE ANNOYING. SURE, SHE'S A LIBERAL, BUT EVA BRAUN, I MEAN THAT'S OVER THE TOP AND IT'S SELF-DISCREDITING, ISN'T IT? I MEAN THAT'S NOT FAIR TO COMPARE TO HITLER'S WIFE." —Tucker Carlson, *Crossfire,* June 27, 2002

"CONSERVATIVE COLUMNIST ANN COULTER RECENTLY DESCRIBED *TODAY* SHOW HOST KATIE COURIC AS 'THE AFFABLE EVA BRAUN OF MORNING TV.' AS THIS REVOLTING QUIP SHOWS, NOT ONLY POLITICIANS BUT ALL PUBLIC FIGURES CAN NOW FIND THEMSELVES SMEARED BY ASSOCIATION WITH HISTORY'S MOST INFAMOUS MASS MURDERER." —Michael Lind, *Washington Post,* October 13, 2002

"[ANN COULTER] CALLED KATIE COURIC THE EQUIVALENT OF HITLER'S MISTRESS." —Joe Conason on *Hardball with Chris Matthews,* August 22, 2003

"NO. 1 'MOST LOATHSOME PERSON IN AMERICA': ANN COULTER. THE MERGER OF BIMBO SEX APPEAL AND NEO-FASCIST VITUPERATION . . . EVA BRAUN MEETS *SEX AND THE CITY.*" —"50 Most Loathsome People in America," *The Beast* (Buffalo), December 2002

Oops—that one was about the whole book, not just the Eva Braun crack, which is very, very bad to call someone, unless you are a liberal drawing on your vast store of originality to proclaim, "No, you are!"

JUNE 2003

The Publication of My Number Two *New York Times* Bestseller *Treason: Liberal Treachery from the Cold War to the War on Terrorism* (Which Sold Even More Than My Number One *New York Times* Bestseller *Slander*)

"EVEN A BOLD EXAGGERATOR LIKE COULTER MAY HAVE BITTEN OFF MORE THAN SHE COULD VOMIT." —James Wolcott, *Vanity Fair,* March 2003 (before *Treason* was released)

". . . HER ILL-INFORMED COMIC DIATRIBES . . . COULTER'S PREVIOUS PERFORMANCES WERE PRAISED BY SOME NOW ON THE ATTACK. . . . [T]HE INDELICATE COULTER HAS CROSSED THE LINE." —Sam Tanenhaus, Slate, July 24, 2003

"THOUGH I HAVE NOT FOUND THE TIME TO SIT DOWN AND READ *TREASON* . . . ANN COULTER MIGHT WANT TO TAKE A LOOK IN THE MIRROR. IF IT WERE NOT FOR MY GREAT-GRANDMOTHER AND OTHERS LIKE HER SHE

WOULD NOT HAVE THE RIGHT TO GO ON
TELEVISION IN HER SLINKY OUTFITS."
—Cliff Schecter, United Press International,
August 25, 2003

"WE FIND A BOOK OUT NOW BY ANN
COULTER CALLING—YOU KNOW, IF YOU'RE A
DEMOCRAT, YOU'RE ALMOST A TRAITOR."
—Senator Tom Daschle (D-S.D.), Democratic
Policy Committee Hearing, October 24, 2003

JUNE 2003
On Joe McCarthy

"REDEFINING McCARTHYISM; OUR STAND:
AUTHOR ANN COULTER'S BID TO RESELL JOE
AS HERO IS A DAMNABLE LIE." —Editorial,
The Arizona Republic, July 14, 2003

"AUTHOR'S DEFENSE OF McCARTHYISM
MISFIRES, ALIENATES MANY ON RIGHT . . .
THE BOOK HAS BEEN GETTING ALMOST
UNIVERSALLY NEGATIVE REVIEWS . . . WITH
SOME OF COULTER'S ALLIES ON THE RIGHT
ABANDONING HER, HOWEVER, PERHAPS THE
AUTHOR OF *SLANDER* AND *TREASON* WILL
CALL HER NEXT BOOK *DESERTED.*" —Kevin
Canfield, *Hartford Courant,* July 18, 2003

"NOW, LIKE THE DEMAGOGUE SHE CELEBRATES, ANN COULTER POSES A FAR GREATER DANGER TO THE RIGHT IN THIS COUNTRY THAN TO THE LEFT." —Paul Greenberg, *Arkansas Democrat-Gazette,* July 31, 2003

FEBRUARY 2004
On Max Cleland

Then there was the Max Cleland episode already covered in **How to Talk to a Liberal (If You Must).** I pointed out that liberals were lying about former Senator Max Cleland's injury in Vietnam being the result of an enemy grenade, sexing up his injuries to better attack Bush. Liberals went mental, and I was denounced on the Senate floor and on many news programs, so I had to point out **again** that liberals were lying. Then they shut up.

Later that year, Teresa Heinz Kerry claimed that she became a Democrat because of my attack on Max Cleland, which would mean she allowed her husband to mortgage her $7 million home to finance his campaign to run as a Democratic candidate for president while she was still a Republican.

"DAVID SIROTA OF THE DEMOCRATIC-LEANING CENTER FOR AMERICAN PROGRESS ON THURSDAY CALLED THE COLUMN 'BEYOND THE PALE.'" —"Criticism of Cleland Stirs Outrage," *Chattanooga Times Free Press,* February 13, 2004

"VILE ANN COULTER SMEARS A WAR HERO." —Joe Conason, *New York Observer,* February 13, 2004

"WHEN [TERESA HEINZ KERRY] CHANGED HER AFFILIATION, IT WASN'T FOR KERRY'S SAKE, SHE SAYS, BUT BECAUSE SHE FELT ALIENATED BY THE INCREASINGLY STRIDENT, DIVISIVE RHETORIC OF THE REPUBLICAN PARTY. . . . [MAX] CLELAND WAS ACCUSED OF BEING 'SOFT' ON HOMELAND SECURITY, AND THE CONSERVATIVE COMMENTATOR ANN COULTER CLAIMED THAT HE HAD CAUSED HIS OWN MUTILATIONS BY MISHANDLING A GRENADE." —Judith Thurman, *The New Yorker,* September 27, 2004

Only a liberal could think that putting on the uniform and going to war is a disreputable, humiliating act that can be redeemed only by being hit with an enemy grenade.

FEBRUARY 2005
On Helen Thomas

Liberals, who claim to be so sensitive to our well-dressed friends when it comes to a joke about a Democrat that has nothing to do with gays, viciously attacked a gay conservative columnist for being gay, a point I made in the column excerpted here:

> **LIBERALS** keep rolling out a scrolling series of attacks on [gay conservative columnist Jeff] Gannon for their Two Minutes Hate, but all their other charges against him fall apart after three seconds of scrutiny. Gannon's only offense is that he may be gay.
>
> First, liberals claimed Gannon was a White House plant who received a press pass so that he could ask softball questions—a perk reserved for **New York Times** reporters during the Clinton years. Their proof was that while "real" journalists (like Jayson Blair) were being denied press passes, Gannon had one, even though he

writes for a Web site that no one has ever heard of—but still big enough to be a target of liberal hatred! (By the way, if writing for a news organization with no viewers is grounds for being denied a press pass, why do MSNBC reporters have them?)

On the op-ed page of the **New York Times,** Maureen Dowd openly lied about the press pass, saying: "I was rejected for a White House press pass at the start of the Bush administration, but someone with an alias, a tax evasion problem, and Internet pictures where he posed like the 'Barberini Faun' is credentialed?"

Press passes can't be that hard to come by if the White House allows that old Arab Helen Thomas to sit within yards of the president. Still, it would be suspicious if Dowd were denied a press pass while someone from "Talon News" got one, even if he is a better reporter.

—**"Republicans, Bloggers, and Gays, Oh My!" 2-24-05**

"DEMOCRATS DENOUNCE COULTER'S SLUR OF THOMAS" —George Weeks, *Detroit News,* March 8, 2005

"LAST WEEK ANN COULTER, A PARTICULARLY VICIOUS COLUMNIST IN THE JOE MCCARTHY MODE, CALLED HELEN 'AN OLD ARAB' AND IMPLIED SHE WAS A SECURITY RISK." —Jack Lessenberry, *Toledo Blade,* March 11, 2005

"WHEN ANN COULTER CALLED THE SENIOR WHITE HOUSE CORRESPONDENT HELEN THOMAS AN 'OLD ARAB' IN A FEBRUARY COLUMN, THE AMERICAN-ARAB ANTI-DISCRIMINATION COMMITTEE (ADC) SPRANG INTO ACTION, LOADING COULTER'S PHONE NUMBER AND THE E-MAIL ADDRESS OF UNIVERSAL PRESS SYNDICATE, WHICH DISTRIBUTES COULTER'S COLUMN, INTO A DIGITAL FORM. TEN MINUTES LATER, CAPITOL ADVANTAGE HAD DELIVERED THE E-MAIL TO 15,000 ADC SUBSCRIBERS. IN LESS THAN TWO WEEKS, THE RELEASE HAD GENERATED 600 PROTEST E-MAILS, TWO ARTICLES IN THE *DETROIT FREE PRESS,* AND SUPPORT FROM TWENTY MEMBERS OF CONGRESS." —Jason Boog, *Columbia Journalism Review,* May 2005/June 2005

JUNE 2006
On the Jersey Girls in My Number One *New York Times* Bestseller *Godless*

With my attacks on the Bush-bashing Jersey Girls I had again—but really this time!— "gone too far." This is just the spicy part from my book, with the bland factual elements of my critique omitted:

AFTER 9/11, four housewives from New Jersey whose husbands died in the attack on the World Trade Center became media heroes for blaming their husbands' deaths on George Bush and demanding a commission to investigate why Bush didn't stop the attacks. Led by all-purpose scold Kristen Breitweiser, the four widows came to be known as "the Jersey Girls." (Original adorable name: "Just Four Moms from New Jersey.") The Jersey Girls weren't interested in national honor, they were interested in a lawsuit. They first came together to complain that the $1.6 million average settlement to be paid to 9/11 victims' families by the government was not large enough.

After getting their payments jacked up, the weeping widows took to the airwaves to denounce George Bush, apparently for not beaming himself through space from Florida to New York and throwing himself in front of the second building at the World Trade Center. These self-obsessed women seemed genuinely unaware that 9/11 was an attack on our nation and acted as if the terrorist attacks happened only to them. The whole nation was wounded, all of our lives reduced. But they believed the entire country was required to marinate in their exquisite personal agony. Apparently, denouncing Bush was an important part of their closure process. These broads are millionaires, lionized on TV and in articles about them, reveling in their status as celebrities and stalked by grief-arazzis. I've never seen people enjoying their husbands' deaths so much. . . .

Mostly the Witches of East Brunswick wanted George Bush to apologize for not being Bill Clinton. Like Monica Lewinsky before her, Breitweiser found impeached president Clinton "very forthcoming." She also found the flamboyant Bush-basher Richard Clarke "very forthcoming." Miss Va-Va Voom of 1968 seemed to think the 9/11 Commission was her nationally televised personal therapy session and as long as government officials issued fake apologies, she could have "closure." (One shudders to imagine how Clinton ministers to four widows.) The rest of the nation was more interested in knowing why the FBI was prevented from being given intelligence about 9/11 terrorists here in the United States more than a year before the attack and would have liked to have top government officials back on the job preventing the next terrorist attack rather than participating in a charade intended to exonerate the Clinton administration.

Needless to say, the Democrat rat pack gals endorsed John Kerry for president. Most audaciously, they complained about the Bush campaign using images from the 9/11 attack in campaign ads, calling it "political propaganda"—which was completely different from the "Just Four Moms from New Jersey" cutting campaign commercials for Kerry. And by the way, how do we know their husbands weren't planning to divorce these harpies? Now that their shelf life is dwindling, they'd better hurry up and appear in **Playboy**.
—*Godless*

Hillary got the party started by calling me "heartless," "vicious," and "mean-spirited." True, it was heartless of me to question whether al Qaeda had specifically targeted the Jersey Girls' husbands and whether the other 2,994 victims were just collateral damage. I should have just told them to "put some ice on that," as Juanita Broaddrick says Hillary's husband did after raping her.

"CONSERVATIVE COMMENTATOR ANN COULTER ISN'T KNOWN FOR MINCING WORDS. BUT NEW YORK SENATOR HILLARY CLINTON AND SOME 9/11 WIDOWS SAY HER LATEST COMMENTARY IS A RANT THAT WENT TOO FAR." —CNN *Headline News,* June 7, 2006

"PATAKI SAYS COULTER COMMENTS WERE 'INACCURATE AND UNFAIR.'" —Associated Press, June 7, 2006

"HAS ANN COULTER GONE TOO FAR? ANN COULTER ATTACKS 9/11 WIDOWS. SHOULD HER BOOK BE BANNED?" —CNN, June 12, 2006

"SOMEONE COMES ALONG AND MAKES A COMMENT THAT GOES OVER THE LINE." —Brian Williams, *NBC Nightly News,* June 7, 2006

"HER HATE-FILLED ATTACK ON OUR 9/11 WIDOWS HAS NO PLACE ON NEW JERSEY BOOKSHELVES." —New Jersey Assembly-women Joan Quigley and Linda Stender calling for book retailers to ban the sale of Coulter's book throughout the state, June 14, 2006

"[T]HIS TIME SHE'S GONE TOO FAR."
—Gene Lyons, *Arkansas Democrat-Gazette,*
June 14, 2006 [At least I wasn't being funded
by Richard Mellon Scaife this time!]

"COULTER HAS MADE A FORTUNE BY MAKING
CONTROVERSIAL, SOMETIMES OUTRAGEOUS
CLAIMS IN HER BEST-SELLING BOOKS. BUT
HAS SHE GONE TOO FAR THIS TIME? WILL
EVEN HER LOYAL READERS BE TURNED OFF
BY HER SUGGESTION THAT 9/11 WIDOWS
ARE—QUOTE—'ENJOYING THEIR HUSBANDS'
DEATHS'?
"MAX, I THINK SHE ACTUALLY HAS GONE
TOO FAR. AND I SAY THAT AS SOMEONE WHO
LIKES HER GENERALLY. AND I THINK IT IS
GOING TO HURT HER BOOK SALES THIS
TIME." —Tucker Carlson, *The Situation with
Tucker Carlson,* June 7, 2006

Godless sold more copies than any of
my other massive bestsellers. If the remarks
in my books are so "controversial" and "outrageous," doesn't that make all the Americans who buy my books a bunch of bigots?
It's interesting that writers whose books
don't sell are willing to slander the Americans

who like my books by leaping to the conclusion that my books sell because of "outrageous remarks" rather than because I write good books. I wonder whether there's some sort of ulterior motive at work . . .

Random Remarks That Upset Liberals

Then there are what we in the writing business call "jokes." If you've ever wondered whether the Democrats have become a bunch of women, consider that they have now formally adopted the feminists' motto: "That's not funny!" These are mostly from various speeches and interviews:

Jack Murtha: The reason soldiers invented fragging.
My only regret with Timothy McVeigh is he did not go to the **New York Times** building.
The rioting Muslims remind us why we have to take seriously the threat that Iran has nukes. . . . What if they start having one of these bipolar episodes with nuclear weapons? . . . I think our

motto should be, post-9/11:
Raghead talks tough, raghead faces consequences.
Someone needs to put rat poison in Justice Stevens's crème brûlée.
We need to execute people like John Walker in order to physically intimidate liberals, by making them realize that they can be killed too.
They Shot the Wrong Lincoln [title of column on Lincoln Chafee].
I was going to have a few comments on the other Democratic presidential candidate, John Edwards, but it turns out you have to go into rehab if you use the word "faggot."

LIBERALS IN UNISON: Waaa! Waaaaa!
Liberal bloggers were especially angry about that Edwards crack. I think the denunciation that hurt the most was from I'mALittleGirlInAPinkPartyDress.com.
Howard Dean called my joke "hate-filled, . . . vile rhetoric." Normally I would defer to

Howard Dean when it comes to hate-filled vile rhetoric, because he knows what he's talking about. But here he was wrong. Also, I notice that Dean didn't make a peep when I said virtually the same thing about Al Gore eight months earlier. Are the Democrats trying to tell us something about Gore?

The raghead crack about Ahmadinejad the year before at CPAC brought the usual round of denunciations and "That's not funny!" exhortations, as indicated by a sampling of the headlines:

"MICHIGAN DEMOCRATIC PARTY CHAIR
[MARK] BREWER DEMANDS THAT
[MICHIGAN REPUBLICAN CHAIR SAUL]
ANUZIS DENOUNCE COULTER'S ETHNIC
SLURS." —Targeted News Service,
February 15, 2006

"UNWARRANTED VIOLENCE CAN NEVER BE
RIGHTEOUS." —Robert Steinback, *Miami
Herald,* February 15, 2006

"DEMOCRATS ASK REPUBLICANS TO
CONDEMN COULTER REMARKS."
—*Arab American News,* February 24, 2006

37

"INTENTIONAL HATE SPEECH DOESN'T EXIST IN A BUBBLE, IT'S DANGEROUSLY INFECTIOUS." —Mallory Rubin, *University Wire*, March 27, 2006

"COULTER'S COLD COMMENTS." —Elizabeth Chapman, *University Wire*, June 21, 2006

"ANN COULTER; EXTREMIST MAKEOVER." —Gaby Wood, *The Advertiser* (Australia), July 29, 2006

"CROSSING THE LINE ISN'T FUNNY." —Ina Hughs, *Knoxville News-Sentinel*, November 2, 2006

How many times can they denounce me? It kind of loses its impact after a while. At some point, you don't even notice liberals yelling at you anymore, sort of like the background noise in a city. The important point to observe, young right-wingers, is how easy it is to attack these people.

Apparently liberals haven't noticed, but Christians think it's macho to be attacked. It's always the same people who characterize puncturing a baby's skull and sucking the brains out a "constitutional right" who rise in self-righteous moral condemnation over some harmless little joke I've told. I'm a rotten sinner (along with the rest of you), but if anything I've ever said in my public commentary constitutes a sin, then Jay Leno is spending eternity with Judas Iscariot for the Dan Quayle jokes alone.

But now the thrill is gone. The liberal lynch mobs and conservative collaborators are beginning to bore me. Even Emmanuel Goldstein in Orwell's **1984** had to put up with only two minutes' hate per day. With me, it's becoming nonstop.

Moreover, I don't mean to be critical, but I think liberals have missed some of my zestier quotes, which is why we've decided to compile this volume.

This is your lucky day, liberals! Here's a handy compilation of my most outrageous statements in an easy-to-use format. Call it **Letters from Beyond the Pale.** Call it **The Portable Hate-Monger.** Whatever. Just carry it with you wherever you go. I wouldn't want to be misquoted at your next Workers Progressive Resistance rally.

I feel like C. Auguste Dupin in Edgar Allan Poe's "The Purloined Letter." With their maddening mentality of obsessing over details, the detectives search for a letter by dividing the suspect's office into a Cartesian graph and examining every crevice. It never occurs to them to look on the desk for the letter.

Similarly, I've got plenty of insults for liberals right in front of their faces. They don't need to pore through my books or tape my every speech. I try to provide grounds for a new outrage right on the covers of my books and in my column each week. Because let's be honest: Between charging up the electric car and trying to find Air America on the radio, liberals don't really have all that much time left for monitoring Ann Coulter.

As I read through these quotes, a few observations occur to me. First, my most frequent quote does not appear at all. That is: "May I please finish my thought, Alan?"

Also, I noticed that I attack New York, the **New York Times**, and Harvard a lot. People often ask me why I attack the **New York Times** when this or that newspaper is worse, so I would just like to make clear that, despite my attacks on these elite liberal institutions, they aren't half as bad as any liberal living in the red states.

I attack the **New York Times** because it is the most articulate expression of loony liberal thought in America today. Also, except for about half of it, it's a terrific paper. As the **Treason Times'**s most loyal reader, I have long wanted to cut an ad for them saying, "As long as you skip the editorial page, the op-ed page, any articles on the front page, and anything with these three words, 'By Frank Rich'—the **New York Times** is America's greatest newspaper!"

All liberals are the enemy, but liberals outside of New York are the loser enemy. The whole point of being a liberal is to live in New York. Liberals consider it nirvana to live in Manhattan, so any liberals not living in New York are obviously too stupid to get jobs there. Even in New York, the worst liberals are the ones who can't afford to live in New York, but have stumbled into rent-controlled apartments.

Duke lacrosse prosecutor Mike Nifong does not live in New York. Tom DeLay prosecutor Ronnie Earle does not live in New York. Ward Churchill does not teach at Harvard. What kind of monster could be a liberal in a fabulous state like Colorado—much

41

less North Carolina or Texas? Answer: the biggest losers on the planet.

There is nothing more sublime than being with red-staters in red states, or as I call it, "visiting America." But these feckless losers want nothing of it. They want to be with Courtney Love.

Most newspapers in the red states—even nice states like Mississippi—are run by loser liberals who rub their foreskin while reading the **New York Times**. The various **Times** wannabes around the country have adopted the **Times's** politics, but don't have the native intelligence to pull it off, so they end up sounding more like Cindy Sheehan than a newspaper written by adults.

Think of the pimply harridan with a kerchief on, shouting, "Bush lied kids died!" at an antiwar rally. The **New York Times** is the erudite version of this person. The red-state newspapers are generally written by this person. While the **Times** is deceptive but frequently accurate, the **Arizona Daily Star** and the **St. Louis Post-Dispatch** are merely the illiterate, fact-free scribblings of lunatics.

Attacking papers like these—or the **Berkshire Eagle** (Pittsfield, Massachusetts), the

Durham Herald-Sun, or the **Arkansas Democrat-Gazette**—would be like kicking a dog, a rabid, toothless dog who is about to die anyway. When I attack, I want to target those with power or influence. This is why, for example, you will not see Keith Olbermann mentioned in this book.

I mention this not only to explain the prominent coverage I give to the **New York Times** but also because I've noticed that loser liberals seem to think they can acquire the savoir faire of Manhattan by adopting the worst aspect of the city—its liberalism. The second-worst aspect of New York City is the traffic, but that doesn't mean you're a cool person if you idle your car in a parking lot in Des Moines for three hours a day.

Remember, Loser Liberals: New York City had Republican mayors from 1993 to 2007. Oh and by the way, in the 2004 election, zip code 10021, Manhattan's Upper East Side, gave more money to Bush than any other zip code in the country.

Red-state liberals ("Loser Liberals") engage in crazy, fascistic behavior hoping to bask in the warm glow of liberal adoration, but New York liberals are disdainful of anyone living in the red states. Red-state liberals are brownnosers toward people who hold them in contempt. They even have contempt for themselves, which they try to disguise by being contemptuous of their neighbors. These are the sort of people who welcomed the Wehrmacht.

These backwoods liberals think they have entered the world of Graydon Carter and **Vanity Fair** by launching snotty attacks against George Bush in the **Bunnychip Gazette.** I promise you: Graydon Carter wants nothing to do with you. Oh maybe he'll humor you for a while—accuse the president of lying and you might get a nice photo spread—but there's a limit. About a month after Durham prosecutor Mike Nifong charged three Duke lacrosse players with rape despite DNA evidence proving that no one on the lacrosse team had had sex with the alleged "victim," he was headed for secular sainthood. When the first two innocent men were indicted, **Newsweek** put their mug shots on its cover. A column in the **Washington Post** on the case began: "She was black, they were white, and race and sex were in the air." The **New York Times** reported on August 25, 2006, that there was "a body of evidence" supporting Nifong's decision to indict. But with the alternative media out there reporting the truth, even smart liberals couldn't carry this hayseed Nifong forever. A year later, liberal deity B. Hussein Obama was calling for a federal investigation into Loser Liberal Nifong.

I make fun of Harvard for the same reason that I attack the **New York Times**: It is an important institution. By contrast, Professor Frank Kauffman of Missouri State University is just a run-of-the-mill jackass.

No professor at Harvard would assign his students the project of writing to the state legislature to demand passage of a bill allowing gay adoption. That is simply a fact. And yet that's exactly what Professor Kauffman of MSU did, providing his students with a draft letter in support of gay adoption for them to copy and then sign and mail to the Missouri legislature. When one student, Emily Brooker, refused to do so, Professor Kauffman filed a grievance against her.

Second- and third-rate colleges in America are now run like Soviet committees after the revolution. Everything that ruined education in America began in the sixties, when liberals replaced something that worked with something that sounded good. As if they were the only people who ever thought of it, half-bright professors at colleges where it was easy to get a job changed the job description of professor from "teaching the basics" to "taking a more activist role in changing society."

Curiously, changing society takes a lot less effort than teaching. **I don't see why teaching should be about me going to work. I think the role of a college professor should be about having hot coeds come to my apartment to watch movies. We don't have to write about the movies— we can sleep together and talk about movies after we're done.**

It is striking to someone who gives a lot of college speeches that the two categories of schools where even liberal students behave with civility are: Southern schools and the Ivy League schools and their equivalent. At Harvard, liberals ask questions; at the University of Arizona, they throw food. The third-tier colleges are churning out the loony-left base of the Democratic Party as

46

the lowest-IQ students are ginned up into a feral rage by half-wits like Ward Churchill.

There are lots of bright students at these colleges—they're usually members of the College Republicans—but the faculties have been taken over by the worst of the Worst Generation. College faculties at the third-tier schools are dominated by people with no knowledge to impart, but who thought they looked cool in a beret and decided to stay on at a college campus.

Fortunately for the Ivy League, the faculties at the better schools weren't so easy for the radicals to storm, which is why at Harvard, they're still teaching Shakespeare, notwith-standing the bard's White Male Heterosexist perspective. However nutty some Harvard professors may be, I promise you, no one with the raw stupidity of Ward Churchill is allowed to teach there.

I suppose we should consider ourselves lucky that our sixties generation sequestered themselves in cushy jobs at bush-league colleges, dying local newspapers, and local DA's offices throughout the South. In Germany, sixties radicals took over the government.

This is why I attack the **New York Times** and Harvard, rather than loser liberals in the red states whose idea of a bold statement is to pass gas in church. I'll get into it with the rulers of your little army. They at least call the shots.

A final observation on these quotes is that they're completely out of context, which is odd inasmuch as it used to annoy me when liberals would take my quotes out of context, removing the lush analytical framework leading up to the smashing crescendo and making it sound as if I were just calling Democrats names.

The title of this book, for example, came from a column about Democrats' opposing the NSA program to listen to phone calls placed to al Qaeda cell phones in the Middle East. I think it would be grounds for impeachment if the president were **not** monitoring those phone calls. My column was titled "Why We Don't Trust You with National Security," and among other searing points, I said:

If the Democrats had any brains, they'd distance themselves from the cranks demanding Bush's impeachment for listening in on terrorists' phone calls to Abu Musab al-Zar-qawi. (Then again, if they had any brains, they'd be Republicans.)

I suppose I could have gravely intoned: **There's a moment when a fanatic's ideology trumps his intellect.** But I think my phrase is punchier. My readers understand. They don't need to pore through an entire homily on the dangers of fanaticism. Not only that, but they are perfectly happy with my calling Democrats names, with or without a larger point.

In early 2007, when the media went on one of their defamation campaigns against me after my Edwards joke at CPAC, I was sorely tempted to interrupt my peace and solitude in order to scream from the rooftops, "I HAD TO USE THE WORD 'FAGGOT' BE-CAUSE THAT'S THE WORD ACTOR ISAIAH WASHINGTON WAS SENT TO REHAB FOR!" If Isaiah Washington had gone into rehab for using the word that rhymes with "basshole," I would have made the same joke about Al Gore. If he had gone into rehab for using the word "bitch," I would have used the same joke for Hilla—no, actually, I think that would have been Edwards again.

But a casual review of reader postings on the Web demonstrated that absolutely no one missed the reference to the Washington story, which had been all over the news about one week earlier, so I went back to floating in the pool. In fact, as far as I could tell, the main point being made by normal Americans was: "Well, Edwards **is** kind of a faggot."

And by the way, while some of my alleged conservative "allies" dearly love joining the increasingly frequent liberal lynch mobs against me in the misguided belief that if only I could be destroyed, perhaps Americans would buy **their** books instead, one group of Americans is unyielding in their defense of the truth through every single attack: my fellow Christians. The more liberals yelp about this or that saucy remark of mine—in between plotting the destruction of the United States of America—the more Christians rally to my defense. This is a fact for which I am eternally grateful. (I am referring here to the vast majority of authentic Christians, not the pious fraud "minister" who attacked me for having once dated Bob Guccione Jr.—the son of a pornographer, who went to church every Sunday, took care of his mother, and created a fabulously successful music magazine with no help from his father. But thanks for your Christian insight, Mr. Pharisee.)

Irritating as liberals are, I'd just as soon have them waste their energy attacking me than burning the flag, writing a national "choice" law, or flying to Alabama to take down another Ten Commandments monument. You can never get to a Christian. We've got nothing to lose that they can take from us. Go ahead and waste your impotent rage on me. Make my day.

So instead of waiting for liberals to take my quotes out of context, I'm taking them out of context myself. Fasten your seat belts! This time, I am going "too far."

AIRPORT SECURITY:
MAKE IMAMS TAKE BUSES

Since flights resumed after the attacks of September 11, 2001, the sounds of the airport have included the tinkle of tweezers being dropped in airport security "weapons" boxes, the patter of bare feet through magnetometers, and hearty shouts of **Step aside, Mohammed, we've got to frisk the blonde chick!** But there's good news, too. It's now virtually impossible to hijack a plane using an oversized carry-on bag or a bottle of Evian water.

[The evidence]

THE men who used passenger jets to attack America on Sept. 11 were Muslim extremists.

Last year, our warship the USS **Cole** was attacked by Muslim extremists.

In 1998, U.S. embassies in Kenya and Tanzania were bombed by Muslim extremists, killing 212 people and wounding thousands.

In 1996, Muslim extremists exploded a truck bomb outside an Air Force housing complex in Saudi Arabia, killing 19 and injuring hundreds more.

In 1995, five Americans were killed in a car bomb explosion executed by Muslim extremists.

In 1993, the World Trade Center was bombed by Muslim extremists, killing six and injuring thousands.

Also in 1993, Muslim extremists plotted to assassinate former U.S. president George Bush. (Intriguingly, the word "assassin" comes from a Muslim sect active in the 11th to 13th centuries known as "the Assassins" for their religious practice of murdering infidels.)

In 1988, another passenger jet, Pan Am flight 103, was bombed by Muslim extremists, killing 270 people.

In 1986, Muslim extremists bombed a West Berlin discotheque frequented by U.S. servicemen.

In 1985, Muslim extremists seized an Italian cruise ship, the **Achille Lauro,** and murdered Leon Klinghoffer, a sixty-nine-year-old, wheelchair-bound American.

In 1983, Muslim extremists blew up U.S. Marine barracks in Beirut, killing 241 American servicemen.

In 1982, Muslim extremists bombed the U.S. embassy in Beirut, killing 49 people, including 17 Americans.

In 1979, Muslim extremists stormed the U.S. embassy in Iran and held American embassy staff hostage for 444 days.

So naturally, it took the airlines completely by surprise last week when the passenger who tried to detonate a sneaker bomb on a passenger jet turned out to be a Muslim extremist. Doggedly imitating an Alzheimer's joke, the airlines instantly began ever more intrusive examinations of elderly black men, cowboys, and Asian women with small children. —"We'll Pay Them Reparations Later," 12-27-01

9/11 commissioner John Lehman revealed that "it was the policy [before 9/11] and I believe remains the policy today to fine airlines if they have more than two young Arab males in secondary questioning because that's discriminatory." Hmmm . . . Is nineteen more than two? —"Thank You for Choosing United, Mr. bin Laden," 4-15-04

[I]N the government's obsessive drive for "equality," perhaps airport security guards will be forced to start searching Arabs now, too. —"Mineta's Bataan Death March," 2-28-02

THE FAA's new hijacker repellent is this: Passengers will now have to show boarding passes to get to the gates. This wily stratagem will stop cold any hijackers on suicide missions who forgot to buy airline tickets. —"Where's Janet Reno When We Need Her?," 9-20-01

SO far, America's response to a calculating cold-blooded enemy has been to say, "Excuse me, you seem to have dropped your box cutter." —**"Future Widows of America: Write Your Congressman," 9-28-01**

THE government's logical calculus on flight security has long been: Really Annoying = Safe Plane. (Does anyone not know how to use a seat belt? Say you were an alien from a distant galaxy and had never in your entire life seen a seat belt before—couldn't you figure it out?) —**"Where's Janet Reno When We Need Her?," 9-20-01**

LIKE many of you, I carefully reviewed the lawsuits against the airlines in order to determine which airlines had engaged in the egregious discrimination [against Muslim men], so I could fly only those airlines. . . . What a wasted marketing opportunity! Imagine the great slogans the airlines could use:

"Now Frisking All Arabs—Twice!"
"More Civil-Rights Lawsuits Brought
    by Arabs Than Any Other Airline!"

"The Friendly Skies—Unless You're an
  Arab!"
"You Are Now Free to Move About the
  Cabin—Not So Fast, Mohammed!"
—"Arab Hijackers Now Eligible For
Preboarding," 4-25-04

ONE hundred percent of the terrorist attacks on commercial airlines based in
America for twenty years have been committed by Muslims. When there is a 100
percent chance, it ceases to be a profile. It's
called a "description of the suspect."
—*Treason*, p. 265

Q: What if the free market offered Muslim-
  free air travel?
A: This is my idea—I'm way ahead of you.
  I think airlines ought to start advertis-
  ing: "We have the most civil rights law-
  suits brought against us by Arabs."
Q: And how would Muslims travel?
A: They could use flying carpets.
  —Interview, *The Guardian* (U.K.), 5-17-03

THE idea that a Muslim boycott against
US Airways would hurt the airline proves

that Arabs are utterly tone-deaf. This is roughly the equivalent of Cindy Sheehan taking a vow of silence. How can we hope to deal with people with no sense of irony? The next thing you know, New York City cabdrivers will be threatening to bathe.
—"What Can I Do to Make Your Flight More Uncomfortable?," 11-22-06

[S]TUDIES have shown that demanding photo ID is a highly effective method of keeping vampires off airplanes. The defect in the photo ID requirement is that terrorists, unlike vampires, are capable of having their photos taken. No one has told the FAA this—but terrorists have ID cards.
—"HillaryCare for the Airports," 11-8-01

TO pull off a 9/11-style attack now, literally half the passengers on the plane would have to be terrorists. (At least the airport screeners wouldn't have to worry about confiscating a lot of deodorants.)
—"Terrorists Win: Deodorant Banned from Airplanes," 8-16-06

Q: What is your overall assessment of President Bush's Homeland Security efforts to date?

A: Not enough racial profiling.
—Carol Devine-Molin, "Interview with Conservative Favorite Ann Coulter," GOPUSA News, 6-10-02

SIX imams removed from a US Airways flight from Minneapolis to Phoenix are calling on Muslims to boycott the airline. If only we could get Muslims to boycott all airlines, we could dispense with airport security altogether. —"What Can I Do to Make Your Flight More Uncomfortable?," 11-22-06

BABY-KILLING: ABORT LIBERALS, NOT CHILDREN

A "moderate Democrat" is someone who experiences doubt when undergoing her third abortion. The party of compassion believes it is very important to have "choice" when it comes to killing babies, but not so important when it comes to what you think about global warming, about which we must have 100 percent uniform belief enforced by left-wing border guards. As First Lady, Hillary Clinton's first order of business was to convene a feminist caucus to draft ever more draconian punishments in her health care plan for peaceful protesters at abortion clinics. **We don't have a lot of time, ladies, so let's get right to punishments for interfering with an abortion**

clinic. Liberals will pass laws to protect children from "secondhand smoke" but not from being doused with poisonous saline solution or having their skulls crushed in the womb. This is why liberals are known as "compassionate."

The same people who think a woman should be able to have an abortion without informing her husband demanded that Terri Schiavo's husband be allowed to kill her while she was in a coma and he was living with another woman. Is it just me, or is the pro-choice cause coming to seem more and more like a pro-man cause?

We crossed a major Rubicon when the pro-abortion crowd finally admitted that abortion was not all sweetness and light. Climbing out of the tree, feminists recently began acknowledging that abortion is evil—albeit a "necessary evil." So pleased with themselves for finally coming up with a response to the "Murder-is-wrong" argument, the pro-aborts began blurting it out constantly: **No one is** for **abortion.**

But of course they are. NARAL believes abortion is a fundamental human right, the sine qua non of women's equality. Isn't everyone **for** fundamental human rights? Isn't everyone **for** women's equality? The "no one is for abortion" line is just rearranging the deck chairs on a sinking argument.

It is not a surprise that the people who most fervently support abortion refuse to discuss it, a condition known as "abortion denial." Of course, it would be tricky to write a caption for those abortion photos, inasmuch as it is prohibited by law to use the word "abortion." **Nurse Smith examines a bucket containing Ms. Jones's choice.**

IF only Democrats could get the American people to believe that a group with the words "abortion" and "rights" in its name is some kind of benevolent little charity that holds bake sales. —"Alito Nominated; Democrats Hide from Base," 11-3-05

[**LIDDY**] Dole has called abortion "the most difficult question there is," which is not only insulting, but incomprehensible to opponents of abortion. If it's a life—as Mrs. Dole claims she believes it is—abortion is a pretty easy question, unless you're Hannibal Lecter. —**"The Stupidity Litmus Test,"** 7-3-00

THE Democrats are trying to "reframe" their message to make people think they believe abortion is wrong. I think this is going to be a hard sell if they plan to continue ferociously defending abortion on demand right up until the moment the baby's head is through the birth canal. — **"Abortion Stops a Bleeding Heart,"** 1-25-06

ABORTION—like other liberal priorities over the years including forced busing, gay marriage, and removing "under God" from the Pledge of Allegiance—is an issue liberals believe is best voted on by groups of nine or fewer. —**"Where's That Religious Fanatic We Elected?,"** 1-27-05

LIBERALS are more upset when a tree is chopped down than when a child is aborted. Even if one rates an unborn child less than a full-blown person, doesn't the unborn child rate slightly higher than vegetation? —*Godless,* p. 5

THIS is the logic of the pro-abortion zealots (aka "the Democratic Party"): Either lift every single restriction on abortion or . . . every woman in America will be impregnated by her father and die in a back-alley abortion! —**"Read My Lips: No New Amnesty,"** 5-17-06

RECENTLY, [Wesley] Clark came out for abortion—for any reason—right up until the moment of birth, thus sewing up the coveted Jack Kevorkian endorsement. —Speech, CPAC, 2-25-03

WE hear a lot about the 2 million people in America's jails and how many of them are black, but we rarely talk about the 35 to 40 million abortions since **Roe v. Wade** and how many of those babies were black. When your position on black abortion is identical to the Klan's, maybe it's time to reconsider. —**"40 Excuses and a Mule,"** 10-27-04

[**DEMOCRATIC**] candidates are willing to sell out any of [their] other issues in service of the secret burning desire of all Democrats: abortion on demand. If they could just figure out a way to abort babies using solar power, that's all we'd ever hear about. —"In Search of the Better 'Phony American,'" 1-22-04

MEN support abortion more than women do. On the basis of casual observation, single men between the ages of eighteen and thirty are strongly supportive of a woman's right to have irresponsible, casual sex with them. —*Godless,* p. 83

WHEN they're running for office, all Democrats claim to support tax cuts (for the middle class), to support gun rights (for hunters), and to "personally oppose" abortion. And then they get into office and vote to raise taxes, ban guns, and allow abortions if a girl can't fit into her prom dress. —"Massachusetts Supreme Court Abolishes Capitalism," 11-27-03

[**DEMOCRATS**] said their ideas were too complex to fit on a bumper sticker. This is crazy. "I ♥ partial birth abortion" fits quite easily. —*Godless,* p. 101

BLACKS: THE ONLY THING STANDING BETWEEN THE DEMOCRAT PARTY AND OBLIVION

To the casual observer, Democrats seem hell-bent on pushing blacks out of their party. Hey—didn't Hispanics just become the largest minority group? What a weird coincidence.

Democrats see blacks not as individuals, but as a voting bloc—and a not particularly bright voting bloc. Endlessly repeating the myth that will not die, in the 2000 presidential campaign, Gore used the three-fifths-of-a-person argument when he was running for president to claim that our forefathers thought blacks didn't "count" as a full person.

As any idiot knows, it was the antislavery framers who didn't want to count blacks as full persons in determining congressional representation. This constitutional provision had nothing to do with slavery or voting; it simply determined congressional apportionment. If blacks counted as full persons, the slave-owning states would have overwhelmed the Congress. And yet you hear about the three-fifths clause on Air America approximately once a week, as if it were a sop to racist Southerners. The slaveholding Southern states would have loved to count blacks as five people—that would have massively increased their power in Congress.

Before attacking conservative blacks, liberals run to the NAACP like they're going to a judge for a warrant:

Can we attack Clarence Thomas and J. C. Watts for being stupid?

"Yes, sure, let me sign the warrant."

Dusting off the playbook from the Clarence Thomas nomination, Democrats disparaged every single black person in authority throughout the Bush administration, generally with nasty insinuations about their intelligence and competence.

Blacks were treated to a very special

round of condescension in 2004, when liberals were disconsolate over some unwarranted criticism of a cartoon sponge and decided to take it out on blacks. Richard Clarke claimed in his Bush-bashing book, **Against All Enemies,** that when he briefed Condoleezza Rice on al Qaeda, she looked perplexed, which he interpreted to mean that she had never heard of al Qaeda. Although Rice had been talking about al Qaeda for years, this struck the media as a totally believable charge. **Sorry, Condi. You failed the literacy test.**

The next year, in 2005, the Democrats did not name Donna Brazile—one of three remaining intelligent Democrats in the entire party, who happens to be black—to head the Democratic National Committee. Instead, Democrats chose the goofy WASP in the green pants, Howard Dean. You couldn't even say, **Yes, but look at all Dean has done for blacks!**

Democrats simply use blacks for their votes and as stalking horses for the causes liberals actually care about, like abortion and sexual harassment laws. They love invoking the majestic phrase "civil rights"—

without allowing follow-up questions. When Democrats start claiming a Republican is bad on "civil rights," I promise you, it has nothing to do with blacks.

In the 1998 Maryland gubernatorial race, for example, Democrats ran an ad exclusively in black neighborhoods claiming that Republican candidate Ellen Sauerbrey had "a civil rights record to be ashamed of." The alleged "civil rights" bill that Sauerbrey had voted against—along with a majority of the Maryland legislature—had nothing to do with blacks. It was a sexual harassment bill. This would be hard to ascertain from the ad, which showed pictures of sad black people.

Democrats love the racist smear, but don't have much interest in promoting actual black people within the Democratic Party. Democrats won't even listen to them. When civil rights heroes supported the nomination of Judge Charles Pickering to a federal appeals court, Democrats ignored them, deferring instead to the hysterical denunciations of Pickering by People For the American Way, based in Malibu. According to liberals living in New York and California—but no black person living in Mississippi—Pickering was a "racist."

Pickering testified against the Klan when he was a young prosecutor in Mississippi, putting his life in danger. He worked with the FBI to stop Klan violence. Unlike any current or former member of People For the American Way, Pickering sent his children to majority black schools. His nomination was supported by several past presidents of the NAACP in Mississippi and apparently every black person who had ever set foot in Mississippi.

But liberals ginned up a phony complaint about Pickering based on a single ruling in which he reduced a wildly disproportionate seven-year sentence for a cross-burner, who wasn't even the ringleader but happened to be stupid enough to be set up as the fall guy. Pickering, a civil rights hero, was smeared as a racist in order to save abortion. Rich white women have suffered so much—more than blacks, apparently. I know that from listening to Democrats.

DEMOCRATS don't care about race discrimination: They are the party of race discrimination! George Wallace, Bull Connor, Bob Byrd—all Democrats! —*Godless,* p. 94

WITH their infernal racial set-asides, racial quotas, and race norming, liberals share many of the Klan's premises. The Klan sees the world in terms of race and ethnicity. So do liberals! —*Slander,* p. 26

Democratic strategist **BOB BECKEL:** I have no problem with [Condoleezza Rice] because she's black. I have a problem with her because I don't think she's up to the job. Do not begin to say that people like me are racist when I spent a lot of time out in the vineyards on the civil rights movement. . . . You've got to be careful here, Ann.
COULTER: And you listen to jazz.
—*Hannity & Colmes,* 11-17-04

THE [John] Kerry campaign is hemorrhaging black voters like teenaged girls fleeing an R. Kelly house party. . . . Kerry waited for complaints that the only black people in

his campaign were setting up folding chairs at rallies before finding blacks for any prominent positions. (Another campaign slogan: "John Kerry: Pretending to Fight for Blacks Since Very Recently.")
—"40 Excuses and a Mule," 10-27-04

IN light of their reaction to the nomination of Condoleezza Rice as secretary of state, I gather liberals have gotten over their enthusiasm for multiculturalist milestones. It's interesting that they dropped their celebrations of the "first woman!" "first black!" "first Asian!" designations at the precise moment that we are about to get our first black female secretary of state. . . . When Madeleine Albright was appointed the FIRST WOMAN secretary of state, the media was euphoric. (And if memory serves, Monica Lewinsky was the first Jewish female to occupy her various positions on the president's, uh, staff.)
—"It's Dr. Rice, Not Dr. Dre," 12-1-04

LIBERALS are going to have to figure out a way to cut [Condoleezza Rice] out of all the pictures. It's going to be like Stalinist Russia:

"Say, who's that black woman standing next to Bush?"

Oh, never mind—it's probably someone he's arresting! It's the maid! —Interview, *New York Observer*, 1-10-05

[T]HE gravest danger facing most black Americans today is the risk of being patronized to death. —*Slander*, p. 1

I BELIEVE more African-Americans spent this season reflecting on the birth of Christ than some phony non-Christian holiday invented a few decades ago by an FBI stooge. Kwanzaa is a holiday for white liberals, not blacks. —"Kwanzaa: Holiday from the FBI," 12-28-05

THE closest black woman to Bill Clinton was his secretary, Betty Currie—whose principal function was penciling in "Monica" on Clinton's "To Do" list every morning. —"It's Dr. Rice, Not Dr. Dre," 12-1-04

AMONG the burdens liberals have placed on blacks is the nutty idea that all blacks are obliged to defend the worst elements of their race. White people don't feel a need to defend Jeffrey Dahmer or Scott Peterson. Go ahead, kill him. . . . In fact, the biggest dilemma we usually face after a case like Scott Peterson's is "Lethal injection, or Old Sparky?" —**"We're the 'Lose-Lose' People!," 12-15-04**

WHAT Democrats mean by "civil rights" is the civil right of a woman not to inform her husband she's aborting his baby; the civil right of a minor to have an abortion without notifying her parents; the civil right of a woman to plunge a fork in the head of a child as it struggles through the birth canal because it has a cleft lip. That's "civil rights." —*Godless*, p. 94

CLINTON actually compares his battle against impeachment to civil rights struggles in the South. Haven't blacks been insulted enough by the constant comparison between gay marriage and black civil rights without this horny hick comparing his impeachment to Selma?
—**"Moby's Dick," 6-23-04**

HERE'S the deal on politics and race in America: Republicans don't need black voters, but they want them. Democrats don't want black voters, but they need them.
—"40 Excuses and a Mule," 10-27-04

IF we can get blacks to be conservatives, we'll have an entire race of Ann Coulters. They do not care about politically correct.
—Interview, *New York Observer,* 1-10-05

GEORGE W. BUSH:
THE GUY I'D MOST LIKE TO HAVE A NONALCOHOLIC BEER WITH

President George W. Bush is evidently the first mentally retarded person to get a Harvard M.B.A., graduate from the U.S. Air Force Flight School, be elected governor of Texas, and then be elected president of the United States twice. I guess this is what they call "mainstreaming." Admittedly, it took Bush two weeks to learn how to pronounce "Shiite," but he had higher grades at Yale than John Kerry. Then again, who didn't?

Q: What will liberals say when George Bush leaves office?

A: They will say, "Many people would like to give George Bush credit for transforming the entire Middle East. But it was inevitable; it was going to happen anyway. It would have happened under John Kerry." —Interview, *New York Observer*, 1-10-05

FOR six years, the Bush administration has kept America safe from another terrorist attack, allowing the Democrats to claim that the war on terrorism is a fraud, a "bumper sticker," a sneaky ploy by a power-mad president to create an apocryphal enemy so he could spy on innocent librarians in Wisconsin. And that's the view of the moderate Democrats. The rest of them think Bush was behind the 9/11 attacks.
—"The 'Bumper Sticker' That Blows Up," 7-18-07

AFTER living through an administration that produced a cornucopia of misogynist and felonious behavior, the very same people who were defending the felons are now beyond indignation about Bush.
—"Hail Mary Past," 11-6-00

GEORGE W. Bush surged in the polls this week in response to reports that Alec Baldwin and Elton John would leave the country if Bush is elected president. —**"So Who's the 'Dumb Guy' Now?,"** 10-3-00

GEORGE Bush with degrees from Yale and Harvard is ridiculed for his stupidity by Hollywood starlets whose course of study is limited to what they've learned from bald sweaty men on casting couches. —*Slander*, p. 125

AFTER years of defending Clinton, liberals love the piquant irony of calling Bush a liar. —**"Pots and Kettles,"** 7-24-03

THE eighteen-month "rush" to war—and still the Democrats didn't have enough evidence that Saddam Hussein was a threat. But they can make a split-second decision that George Bush is a threat. —*Hannity & Colmes*, 11-17-04

[L]IBERAL hysteria always frightens Bush. Instead of poking them through the iron

bars of their cages with a stick like a normal person would, Bush soothes them with
food pellets and reassuring words. What
fun is that? We're winning! This is no time
to concede defeat. —"Actually, 'Judicial Activism' Means 'E = mc²,' " 9-14-05

IF George W. Bush announced that a cure
for cancer had been discovered, Democrats
would complain about unemployed labo-
ratory rats. —"It's Like Christmas in December," 12-18-03

[Responding to a Bush malapropism]
AND we kicked your butt in two presiden-
tial elections with that guy. —*Hannity &
Colmes,* 11-2-06

WHAT on Earth was President Bush doing
announcing to everyone in a State of the
Union address that one of his father's favorite people was Bill Clinton? I wonder
how Juanita Broaddrick was enjoying that
part of the speech. Who exactly is that
supposed to impress? The Republican
president who raised our taxes and was

thrown out after one term likes an impeached multiple felon. Who's Papa Bush's other favorite person? Harry Belafonte?
—Speech, CPAC, 2-10-06

COLMES: Are all the American people that don't support [Bush] dumb?
COULTER: No. I think, as I indicated in my last book, they're traitors.
—*Hannity & Colmes*, 6-23-04

CHRISTIANS: MUST REPRODUCE MORE

Political campaigns are always a lot of fun because we get to see Democrats pretend to believe in God and take a stab at which testament contains the Book of Job. If you don't think Democrats have a problem with voters who believe in God (as opposed to "believe" in "God"), consider that in 2004, Bush won more of the traditionally Democratic Catholic vote than John Kerry, who purports to be a Catholic. Then again, Kerry also claimed to be a war hero, and war heroes didn't vote for him either.

At this stage, it looks as if the Democrats have finally hit on the perfect presidential candidate for 2008: B. Hussein Obama. He's black and white and has a Muslim, atheist, and Christian background. So **all** Democrats can be happy with B. Hussein Obama. Liberals can vote for the atheist, Bob Byrd Democrats can vote for the white guy, Black Muslims can vote for, well . . . the Black Muslim, and African-Americans can vote for Hillary.

IF I knew as little about Islam as [liberals] know about American Christians, I would be guilty of a hate crime. —*The O'Reilly Factor,* 10-3-06

CHRISTIANITY is even more important to me than homosexuality is to liberals— which apparently comes in a close second to defending Saddam Hussein and preaching anti-Semitism.
—Interview, *The Guardian* (U.K.), 5-17-03

IF you want something that complicates a belief in God, try coming to terms with Michael Moore being one of God's special creatures. —*Godless,* p. 199

ACCORDING to liberals, the message of Jesus, which somehow [Mel] Gibson missed, is something along the lines of "be nice to people." . . . In fact, Jesus' distinctive "message" was: People are sinful and need to be redeemed, and this is your lucky day because I'm here to redeem you even though you don't deserve it and I have to get the crap kicked out of me to do it. That is the reason He is called "Christ the Redeemer" rather than "Christ the Moron Driving Around in a Volvo with a 'Be Nice to People' Bumper Sticker on It."
—"The Passion of the Liberal," 3-3-04

[**HOSTAGE** Ashley] Smith saved the soul of a man on a killing spree by talking to him about Christianity. But liberals think this won't work with the Muslims? We ought to fly this Ashley Smith to Saudi Arabia. We could just make her a box lunch every day and send her on her way.
—"The Purpose-Driven Left," 4-6-05

BY showing him genuine Christian love, Smith turned [Brian] Nichols from a beast to a brother in Christ. This phenomenon, utterly unknown to liberals, is what's known as a "miracle." Top that, Paul Krugman! —"The Purpose-Driven Left," 4-6-05

Q: [W]hy the liberal obtuseness when it comes to understanding the role religion plays in American history and among Americans in general?

A: They aren't obtuse, they understand religion just fine. They just don't like it. It's not a failure of comprehension. Liberals hate the idea of God because it competes with their conception of themselves as a specially anointed elite. —Interview, *Insight* magazine, 9-16-03

LIBERALS are constantly accusing Christians of being intolerant and self-righteous, but the most earnest Christian has never approached the preachy intolerance of a liberal who has just discovered a lit cigarette in a nonsmoking section. —*Godless*, p. 17

IT'S no wonder Bible Belt, right-wing Christians get the greatest enjoyment out

of sex (another scientific study hated by liberals)—they never have to endure listening to liberals talk about sex.
—*Godless*, p. 14

THE ACLU along with the Southern Poverty Law Center sued [Judge Roy] Moore for having a Ten Commandments plaque in his courtroom. (Poverty had been nearly eliminated in the South until a poor person happened to gaze upon Moore's Ten Commandments—and then it was back to square one.) —**"Place Your Right Hand on the Koran and Repeat After Me," 1-2-04**

THERE is no surer proof of Christ's divinity than that he is still so hated some two thousand years after his death. —**"It's the Winter Solstice, Charlie Brown!," 9-25-03**

IT is constantly the blue states oppressing the red states, not the red states oppressing the blue states. It's not like Jerry Falwell is flying to New York and going over the schools' curriculum, demanding that we shut down the Halloween parade. To the

contrary. It's Malibu and New York and their buddies on the Supreme Court saying, "No prayers in school! No Ten Commandments in the court! Abortion must be legal everyplace!"
—Interview, Salon, 7-25-03

IT'S become increasingly difficult to distinguish the pronouncements of the Episcopal Church from the latest Madonna video. —Interview, Beliefnet, 7-26-06

BELIEFNET: Do you attend church frequently? Do you pray, and whom and what do you pray for?

COULTER: Yes and yes. I pretend to attend a giant church in New York City, where I pray for the souls of people who claim I've never been there. I pray for mercy and divine protection from God's enemies. When I'm in a jaunty mood, I pray for Him to smite liberals.
—Interview, Beliefnet, 7-26-06

CHRISTIANS who are willing to leave the safety and comfort of America to go to bar-

barous lands, risking disease, pestilence, and murder, simply because they so love their fellow man—these are the miscreants who inflame and enrage liberals more than Saddam Hussein and his rape rooms ever did. —**"Will the True Imperialist Religion Please Stand Up?," 4-25-03**

FOX News's Bill O'Reilly refuses to show the [Muslim] cartoons on **The O'Reilly Factor,** saying he doesn't want to offend anyone's religion. Someone should tell him those endless interviews with prostitutes from the Bunny Ranch and porn stars aren't high on Christians' list of enjoyable viewing either. —**"So Three Muslims Walk into a Port," 3-20-06**

LIKE many popular clichés, the opposition to "organized religion" is an utterly meaningless formulation. There are boatloads of religions and thousands of ways religion is organized and practiced. If absolutely none of them float your boat, it may not be a problem of organization.
—*Slander,* p. 184

BELIEFNET: Are churches that don't agree with your politics or religious beliefs not really churches?

COULTER: Correct: They're called "mosques."

—Interview, Beliefnet, 7-26-06

BILL CLINTON: HE LEFT A MARK ON HISTORY THAT MAY NEVER COME OUT

Some say Bill Clinton's most memorable line was "I did not have sex with that woman—Monica Lewinsky." But this trivializes the Clinton presidency. His true epitaph will be "You better put some ice on that."

Fun Word Facts About Inaugural Speeches
Abraham Lincoln's second inaugural address: used the word "God" fourteen times.
Ronald Reagan's second inaugural address: used the words "free" or "freedom" nineteen times.
Bill Clinton's second inaugural address: used the word "consensual" sixteen times.

CLINTON'S library is the first one to ever feature an Adults Only section. —Speech at the University of Texas-Austin, 5-4-05

A PRESIDENT who is so lacking in virtue that a V-chip is required to discuss his conduct in office surely warrants the impeachment remedy. —*High Crimes and Misdemeanors*, p. 269

LIBERALS' idea of intellectual engagement is Bill Clinton's adolescent cramming in all-night slumber parties, leaving the place littered with pizza rinds and women's panties. —*Slander*, p. 135

O.J. [**WAS**] the model for Clinton's second term. He has no alibi, no story whatsoever, and he has left a trail of DNA across a string of Jane Does. He just says he didn't do it and refuses to explain anything further. —*High Crimes and Misdemeanors*, p. 106

CLINTON'S defense [was] essentially that he is not impeachable because his conduct is so disreputable that the framers could not have conceived of it. —*High Crimes and Misdemeanors,* p. 105

COLMES: Tell me if you think this is over the top. Back when Bill Clinton was president, here's what [Congressman] Dan Burton had to say . . . "If I could prove 10 percent of what I believe happened, he'd be gone. This guy's a scumbag. That's why I'm after him." Is that over the top?

COULTER: I don't know. Do you disagree that he's a scumbag?

COLMES: Is that over the top?

COULTER: Do you disagree that he's a scumbag?

COLMES: Don't answer my question with a question.

COULTER: But I think that gets to the heart of it. Do you disagree with him factually?

COLMES: Yes, I disagree with him factually. Does that . . .

COULTER: Do you?

COLMES: Ann, you're ducking my question. Is it or is it not over the top?

COULTER: I think it's factually correct.

I don't think you could win a slander suit on that.

Democratic consultant **JENNY BACK-US**: There you go again. It's a double standard. It is, it's a double standard for the Republicans.

COULTER: Wait, that man raped a woman.

COLMES: That's not been proven.

COULTER: He molested interns in the White House and lied about it—and you're trying to compare that to going to war in Iraq, which your presidential candidate voted for?

—*Hannity & Colmes*, 5-20-04

A MEMBER of law enforcement recently told me about an interesting serial rapist case in the Washington, D.C., area (not the president). While tying up one of his prospective victims—who escaped harm, by the way—the rapist engaged in casual chitchat, asking the woman what she thought about Clinton. She said she thought he was disgusting. The rapist said, **Yeah, I think so, too.** —"Impeachment

Wrap: The Good, the Bad, and the Lying Scumbag President," 2-11-99

"CLINTONESQUE" is an adjective meaning "oily dissembler, shunned by decent society." —**"Condit Hits Another 'Home Run'!,"** 8-30-01

I SHALL dispense with Clinton's most renowned lies. (Every Democrat commits adultery and lies about it. Fine, they've convinced me.) Clinton also lied every time he said "God bless America" though he doesn't believe in God or America, and I don't recall any Republican ever ripping his skin off about that. —**"Pots and Kettles,"** 7-24-03

CLINTON'S position is that the [Marc] Rich pardon "wasn't worth the damage to my reputation"—which was unblemished until then. Rich deserved a pardon, but if he had to do it over again, Clinton would have withheld the pardon solely to protect his own reputation. —**"Not Moving On, Part II,"** 4-11-02

Q: What mistakes do you think Independent Counsel Kenneth Starr made in his investigation of President Clinton?

A: He didn't stay to pursue the death penalty.
—Interview, American Enterprise Institute, 2004

BILL Clinton will be revered in history books as the George Washington of his day who, along with patriots Larry Flynt and James Carville, "saved the Constitution." He will be honored with a memorial larger than the Washington Monument (though probably the same general design). —*Treason,* p. 13

A CHINESE condom manufacturer recently named one of its condoms the "Clinton," a fitting tribute to the man who had Monica Lewinsky perform oral sex on him in the Oval Office on Easter Sunday. Their advertising slogans are "Always wear a 'Clinton' when you're getting a 'Lewinsky'!"; "I still believe in a place called the G-spot"; "Extra-thin skinned!";

"For when you really, really want to feel her pain." —"What Would Reagan Do?," 9-21-05

THE history books can already record that Clinton is the first sitting president ever to face disbarment proceedings. He's really rounding out his list of "firsts": the first president to have his semen analyzed by the FBI, the first president to have his capacity to induce orgasm described on national TV, the first president to use White House sinks as sexual aids, the first president to be accused of rape within two weeks of being acquitted in an impeachment trial, and, well, the list goes on. —"Too Corrupt to Be an Arkansas Lawyer," 5-30-02

I DIDN'T particularly mind [Clinton's] policies, largely because he didn't have any—if you don't count felony obstruction of justice. —Interview, *The Guardian* (U.K.), 5-17-03

[R]OUGHLY half of Clinton's memoir— hundreds and hundreds of pages—is about every picayune detail of his life before becoming president. Through sheer force of will I shall resist the urge to refer to this book as a "blow by blow" account of Clinton's entire miserable existence. —**"Moby's Dick," 6-24-04**

NOW it is a laugh to read Alexander Hamilton's calm assurance in Federalist no. 68 that the president would always be a virtuous man. —*High Crimes and Misdemeanors,* **p. 314**

AFTER all other suitable office space in Manhattan had dried up—and also after spending the weekend golfing in an all-white club in Florida—Clinton announced he would take an office in Harlem. [T]hat should be nice: Having escaped a mugging on the way to work, Clinton's female employees will then have to face an accused rapist in the office. —**"Clinton Does the Harlem Shuffle," 2-15-01**

DONAHUE: You're proud of what you did to Bill and Hill, aren't you? You impeached the guy.

COULTER: Thank you. You're one of the few who will give me credit for that. —*The Phil Donahue Show,* 7-18-02

I THINK it's useful to see Monica on TV as often as possible, and to remember that President Clinton spent more time meeting with this nitwit hussy than he did with the director of the CIA. —*American Morning with Paula Zahn,* 7-18-02

WELL it looks like John Kerry, John Edwards, and Howard Dean have emerged from the Iowa caucuses in a three-way race. When Bill Clinton heard the news he said, "You know, I remember my first Iowa three-way like it was yesterday." —**Speech,** CPAC, 2-25-03

ON Fox News Sunday with Chris Wallace in September 2006, Wallace asked former president Clinton why he didn't do more to capture bin Laden when he was president. Clinton erupted in a sociopathic rage worthy of an Air America caller. Veteran Clinton watchers said the last time his face was that red there was a chubby intern kneeling in front of him.—*Godless* (paper-back), p. 284

WHAT actually happened during the Clinton presidency? No one can remember anything about it except the bimbos, the lies, and the felonies. Fittingly, in the final analysis, Clinton will not be remembered for what he did as president, but for who he did. —"Moby's Dick," 6-24-04

COLMES: Why would you call the column that? It is obscene. . . . I mean, a conservative who promotes family values and you name the column "Moby's **blank**." Why would you do that?

COULTER: Why would I do that? I did that because I'm writing about Bill Clinton. You may remember that year.

COLMES: But that's really an obscene title. I'm just amazed that you would do something like that.

COULTER: This you're shocked about, but the president of the United States using an intern as an ashtray, raping a woman . . . that was defensible?
—*Hannity & Colmes,* 6-23-04

Q: What should we remember about Bill Clinton?

A: Well, he was a very good rapist. I think that should not be forgotten.

—Interview, *New York Observer,* 1-10-05

HILLARY CLINTON: THE SMARTEST WOMAN IN THE WORLD!

Hillary wants to be the first woman president, which would also make her the first woman in a Clinton administration to sit behind the desk in the Oval Office instead of under it. According to polls, a majority of Americans don't believe the country is ready for a woman president. But the good news is the polls also show that most Americans don't view Hillary as a woman. Hillary's second-biggest accomplishment is having been the First Lady. Her first-biggest accomplishment is not realizing that there was a second, third, fourth, and fifth lady.

WHILE Hillary is certainly qualified to comment on what the all-time worst presidential administrations were, having had firsthand experience in one of them, I think she might want to avoid the phrase "go down in history." —"'Chocolate City' Sprinkled with Nuts," 1-19-06

I THINK Hillary's in a little bit of a tight spot. She's either maintaining that she is, you know, a manipulative liar when she says the first time she found out Bill was fooling around was the night before his grand jury testimony, or she's someone who shouldn't be allowed anyplace near the Oval Office if she is that stupid and naïve. —*Hannity & Colmes,* 6-6-03

JOHN HAWKINS: If you had to name five people on the American left who you found most contemptible, who would they be?

COULTER: Right off the top of my head I'd say Bill and Hillary Clinton and Hillary's three ghostwriters. —Interview, *Right Wing News,* 6-03

[**HILLARY'S** book should] include chapter titles like these: "Where I Hid the Billing Records," "What My Aides Took Out of Vince Foster's Office," "What It's Like to Testify Before a Grand Jury," "Best Velocity for Lamps," and "Hillary's Cattle Futures Trading Tips." —**"Channeling Jackie O,"** **12-21-00**

NEITHER Hillary nor her husband questioned that she had used the phrase "f-ing bastard," only that she would have identified the ethnicity of the f-ing bastard. Even when she's throwing lamps and cursing like a sailor, she's ethnically sensitive. —**"Hillary's Potty Mouth," 8-4-00**

VERNON Jordan had set up a $40,000-a-year job for [Monica] Lewinsky with Revlon—whose parent company had seen fit to hire [Clinton friend and appointee Webster] Hubbell as a consultant for $60,000. Familiarity with the president's private parts apparently had a considerably weaker market value than familiarity with Mrs. Clinton's law practice. —*High Crimes and Misdemeanors*, p. 206

SO Hillary Clinton thinks the House of Representatives is being "run like a plantation." And, she added, "you know what I'm talkin' about." First of all: Think about what a weird coincidence it is that Hillary would have made these remarks in a black church in Harlem on Martin Luther King Day. What are the odds? Did she even know it was a holiday? Bravely spoken, Senator. —" 'Chocolate City' Sprinkled with Nuts," 1-17-06

Q: Was the timing of the release of **Treason** related to when Hillary's book was coming out?

A: Hillary's got a book coming out? You're kidding? I didn't hear a thing about it! Actually I waited a week just to give Hillary a chance to read her own book. —Interview, *Right Wing News,* 6-03

HILLARY Clinton said **Godless** should have been named **Heartless.** I was **mean** to the Jersey Girls. Before Hillary refers to other people being mean to women, she should talk to her husband—who was accused of rape by Juanita Broaddrick and was groping Kathleen Willey simultane-ously with her own spouse committing sui-cide. Maybe she should talk to her husband about being mean to women. —*Hannity & Colmes*, 6-7-06

JOY BEHAR: Do you like to watch two women getting it on?

COULTER: Uh, no. The last time I did was the Katie Couric interview with Hillary Clinton.

—*The View*, 6-25-03

COLLEGES: THE ENGLISH TRANSLATION OF "MADRASSA"

The only successful assaults on Americans' basic freedoms have come from the Left, most spectacularly on college campuses. It is now common for campuses to set aside specifically designated areas known as "free-speech zones," which used to comprise a somewhat larger zone known as "the United States of America."

Liberals vaguely claim to oppose college hate-speech codes, but I notice that the speech codes still exist. All speech is disallowed, except where it is expressly allowed. The speech codes have become such an embarrassment that many colleges now prefer to claim that they are not restricting speech, but rather "verbal conduct" that fosters a "hostile or offensive environment," "interferes with students' ability to learn," or "stigmatizes or degrades" minority groups. So it's not "speech" that is banned, it's just speech that liberals find "hostile" that is banned.

As I learned, for example, apparently it is hate speech and a violation of campus policy to call Teddy Kennedy a "human dirigible" at the University of St. Thomas in Minnesota. So keep that in mind if you're ever speaking there.

I KEEP picking up the **New York Times** and reading about how smart liberals are, and you know, how upset they are that George Bush lacks nuance and he lacks intellectual curiosity. But I go to college campuses. We've got mikes in the audience. Stand up. Show me some of that intellectual curiosity. And they throw food. . . . I note that you don't see any conservatives throwing pies at Michael Moore—and he's asking for them. —*Tonight Show with Jay Leno,* 5-10-05

I LOVE College Republicans because they're so antiauthority. They love annoying their professors. They love annoying the sort of politically correct status quo on campus. And apparently, one popular way of annoying liberals is bringing me to speak. —*Booknotes,* 8-11-02

WHEN contemplating college liberals, you really regret once again that John Walker [Lindh] is not getting the death penalty. We need to execute people like John Walker in order to physically intimidate liberals, by making them realize that they can be killed, too. Otherwise, they will be outright traitors. —**Speech, CPAC,** 2-2-02

Q: Do you regret saying that?
A: Only that I didn't say it loud enough and in a large enough public forum. And when I said we should "execute" John Walker Lindh, I misspoke. What I meant to say was "We should burn John Walker

Lindh alive and televise it on prime-time network TV." My apologies for any misunderstanding that might have occurred.
—Interview, *Right Wing News*, 6-16-06

IN addition to racist and Nazi, how about adding traitor to the list of things that professors can't be? And yes, I realize I just proposed firing the entire Harvard faculty.
—Speech, CPAC, 2-18-05

GIBSON: [A]re you surprised that at Columbia University they're having S&M seminars?

COULTER: Well, it's better than a lot of things they're being taught at Columbia, so it's not all bad news.
—*The Big Story with John Gibson*, 11-28-06

I REALLY think you should get a picture of the members of these [College Sex] clubs and a picture of the young College Republicans and the Christians, because someone who needs to join a club at college to find a way to have sex, probably not your lookers. —*The Big Story with John Gibson*, 11-28-06

HANNITY: What should happen to people that are attacking speakers like you, and [Pat] Buchanan, and [Bill] Kristol, and David Horowitz? What should happen to them?

COULTER: On the basis of what happened to the ones that physically attacked me, I hope they try it again.

HANNITY: Jail time?

COULTER: No. Apparently, the College Republican women gave them a beating they won't forget.
—*Hannity & Colmes*, 5-4-05

IF you want liberalism to continue in this country—I don't, but just to give you a little tip—liberal students are being let down by their professors, by the world. They're buffeted by a liberal media. They have liberal public school teachers. They go to college, they have liberal professors. They don't know how to argue. They can't put together a logical thought, whereas you could put a College Republican on TV right now and he can debate you and do a creditable job. But liberals, they throw food. —*Hannity & Colmes*, 5-4-05

FORTUNATELY for me, liberals not only argue like liberals, they also throw like girls. —"It's Only Funny Until Someone Loses a Pie," 4-13-05

PEOPLE who have dedicated their lives to exposing lesbian imagery in **Moby-Dick** are more prevalent on the nation's campuses than serious scholars. The nation's colleges and universities have become a Safe Streets program for traitors and lunatics. —"We'll Let You Know When You're Being Censored," 7-10-03

CONSERVATIVES from elite schools have already been subjected to liberal blandishments and haven't blinked. These are right-wingers who have fought off the best and the brightest the blue states have to offer. . . . To paraphrase Archie Bunker, when you find a conservative from an elite law school, you've really got something. —"This Is What 'Advice and Consent' Means," 10-5-05

TODAY'S college liberals ape the beliefs of 99 percent of their professors and then pretend they're on-the-edge radicals. —"Apple-Polisher Shows P.O.W. Real Courage," 5-24-06

THE only violence on college campuses these days occurs when people like David Horowitz and me show up to give a speech in defense of America. Then we need bomb-sniffing dogs and a lecture hall lined with armed police. But a Talibanist goes about his day at Yale unmolested. —"Conservatives Need 12-Step Program to Manhood," 5-10-06

COLMES: I keep hearing, oh my, heavens, these people are going to madrassas, if we could only expose them to democracy. So now we have an opportunity to expose this person to democracy, to Yale University of all places, and I keep hearing complaints—
COULTER: I haven't said that.

COLMES: So wouldn't you rather have them in a democratized society?

COULTER: You haven't heard that from me. If we're trying to get these people to love democracy and respect America, the last place I would send them is to an American university.

—*Hannity & Colmes,* 3-13-06

I LOVE to engage in repartee with people who are stupider than I am. —Q&A, University of Connecticut, 12-7-05

COLMES: Did you not treat fellow audience members with dignity in your responses?

COULTER: Far more dignity than their questions deserved.

—*Hannity & Colmes,* 5-4-05

COMMUNISM:
A NEW FRAGRANCE BY
HILLARY CLINTON

We are endlessly bombarded with the idea that the fifties was a frightening era and that Communists were harmless idealists. This is like David Duke referring to his Klan days as a time when he was "idealistic."

Being a Communist for much of the last century was not a theoretical matter. Communists working in Democratic administrations in the thirties, forties, and fifties had a profound influence on which countries would fall under Communist control. This was not like worrying about the sexual orientation of someone working at the State Department. Communism did a lot of bad things. The USSR ruined Eastern Europe, which was not exactly East Timor. These were sophisticated

113

countries. The Soviet conquest of Eastern Europe consisted of backwoods savages conquering sophisticated civilizations.

And the Democrats were rooting for the savages. Thanks to brave American patriots like Joe McCarthy, today Communists in America are substantially less likely to be employed in the Code Room of the Pentagon. These days, they all seem to be kept women, scribbling little essays and living off wealthy spouses or family inheritances. (It's no wonder they take such umbrage at denunciations of the welfare state. They take it personally.)

Communists decided that, first, they would take over education and the media. Education would be the easiest, since it required no skills or talent. Second, they would accuse their opponents of being kooks and nuts. This is the Left's famous psychiatric defense. If you raise an embarrassing point, it's like being at a feminist meeting: **Why would you ask that?**

As Frederick L. Schuman wrote in the **New Republic,** "Underneath their skin, communism and liberalism are blood brothers." The main exception being that the

114

Daily Worker at least had a decent sports page.

We now have a political party in America that supports officially lying about Communism. When the Clinton administration seized Elián González in a machine-gun raid in 2000 in order to send him back to a Communist dictatorship, liberal flack Eleanor Clift said, "Frankly, to be a poor child in Cuba may, in many instances, be better than being a poor child in Miami." The Democrats' Hollywood contingent pals around with Fidel Castro and their new crush, Hugo Chavez, Communist dictator of Venezuela. Just as Republicans have a social-conservative wing, a free-trade wing, and a neoconservative wing, the Democrats have a traitor wing.

For more than fifty years, Democrats have harbored traitors, lost wars, lost continents to Communism, hobnobbed with the nation's enemies, counseled retreat and surrender. As Joe McCarthy said, if liberals were merely stupid, the laws of probability would dictate that at least some of their decisions would serve America's interests. (In other words, given an infinite number of ideas, eventually one of them will actually be a good one, which is also, incidentally, how TV networks choose their fall lineups.)

This is why liberals try to delegitimize impertinent questions about their intentions in foreign policy and try to anathematize people who remind them what they said yesterday.

COMMUNISM is like vegetarianism in that it's actually not very healthy for most people but leftists continue to defend it because it seems like the thing to do.
—Interview, *Right Wing News*, 6-03

Q: Why shouldn't we think of [Harry] Truman as one of the winners of the Cold War?

A: Because, like most things liberals say, it's untrue. Wasn't there a guy named Ronald Reagan who did something about the Cold War? Win it or something? Giving Truman credit for winning the Cold War is like saying Herbert Hoover won World War II because men like Dwight Eisenhower came out of

Hoover's military. . . . [Truman] promoted known Soviet spies to positions of influence after having been warned they were Soviet spies. He denounced the investigation of Soviet spy Alger Hiss as a "red herring." He responded to Winston Churchill's historic Iron Curtain speech by inviting Stalin to come to America to give a rebuttal speech.
—Interview, *Insight* magazine, 9-16-03

LIBERALS titter about conservatives imagining Communists under every bed, while they hysterically claim to see racists under every bed. If, in addition to murdering tens of millions of people, Stalin had maintained "Whites only" water fountains, America would now celebrate a national Joe McCarthy Day. —*Treason*, p. 194

CLAIMING to have been "blacklisted" is Hollywood's version of coming over on the Mayflower. —*Treason*, p. 76

[A]BOUT two hundred people in America were blacklisted from a single frivolous industry. They could still go to Paris or sell

117

real estate or do any number of things. They just couldn't work in the movies. That was the only price they paid for shilling for a mass murderer. —*Treason,* p. 81

Q: Do you think the Left has largely gotten a pass for being so completely, utterly, and entirely wrong about the effects of Reagan's decision to abandon détente and challenge the Soviet Union?
A: The fact that there still is a Democratic Party proves that.
—Interview, *Right Wing News,* 6-03

ELIÁN González spent last Saturday night at a dinner party at the home of major Democratic fundraisers in Georgetown. Must have been a barrel of laughs for a six-year-old. But this was an important engagement: Time is running short on acclimating Elián to life under a Communist dictator, and a Georgetown dinner party was just the place to start. —"Asylum from Georgetown," 5-9-00

CONSERVATIVES are openly blackballed in all the liberal professions—publishing,

Hollywood, the mainstream media, education, and college faculties. Apparently, that's not "blacklisting." It is churlish for conservatives to complain about private censorship. True blacklisting occurs only when someone scowls at a liberal. —**"We'll Let You Know When You're Being Censored," 7-10-03**

ANN COULTER: MY QUOTES ABOUT ME!

Off the record to all reporters planning to interview me: Characterize me as a difficult interview. I don't talk about my boyfriends, my home, what I TiVo, or how I frolicked as a child. This is why I will be unable to recall how many times I almost got married but will remember the precise number of times the **New York Times** ran a photo of President George H. W. Bush throwing up in Japan. (Two.) That's how WASPs deflect irritating personal questions. There's not much in my life that is interesting from a consumer standpoint. If you want more on that, talk to my father. When I came in after midnight as a teenager, I was also a difficult interviewee. These are my answers to questions about ME.

Q: What do you say to your critics who claim that you attack liberals just as viciously as you say conservatives are attacked by liberals?
A: Our insults are true.
  —Interview, *Right Wing News*, 6-03

I AM the illegal alien of commentary. I will do the jokes that no one else will do. —The O'Reilly Factor, 6-28-07

COLLEGE STUDENT: What personally happened in your life to make you so hateful of minorities and the gay community?
COULTER: What did it take in your life to become such a sensitive pantywaist?
  —Interview, Syracuse University, 3-8-06

Q: What would a shrink suggest lay at the root of your hard-core conservatism?

A: Is the shrink a patriotic American? He'd say I'm just fine.
   —Interview, *The Guardian* (U.K.), 5-17-03

I NEVER got the hang of being scared of liberals. The technical term for conservatives who are not afraid of liberals is "unpublished." —*How to Talk to a Liberal (If You Must)*, p. 323

Q: Many liberals that are rich come from the East Coast, are white, had studied at the Ivy university. You are rich (I hope), come from Connecticut, are white, and studied at Cornell. Why do you hate the liberals?

A: Because I know so many of them. Liberals are clueless, amoral sexual degenerates, Communists, and pacifists—no offense to you or your readers intended, of course.
   —Interview, *Il Foglio* (Italy), 10-04

Q: What is your all-time favorite movie and why?

A: **Dr. Strangelove.** Because I think we need more generals like Buck Turgid-

son. And that final scene where our nuclear warhead takes out a Soviet city is priceless! Hey, I'm a sucker for happy endings.
—Interview, American Enterprise Institute, 2004

I HAD happily married parents, a warm and loving family, and a happy childhood with lots of friends. Thus, there were no neurotic incidents to turn me into a liberal. —Interview, FrontPage Magazine, 1-12-04

Q: How would your career be different if you looked like Molly Ivins?
A: I'd be a lot uglier.
—Interview, *Baltimore Sun,* published in "What I Did on My Summer Vacation," 8-2-06

Q: Are you a Christian?
A: Are you a moron? Yes, of course. Where'd you think I got that zesty stuff about abortion and traditional marriage? **The Nation** magazine? The Koran?
—Interview, Citizenlink, 10-19-04

I'M a Christian first and a mean-spirited, bigoted conservative second, and don't you ever forget it. You know who else was kind of "divisive" in terms of challenging the status quo and the powers-that-be of his day? Jesus Christ. —Interview, *Baltimore Sun*, 7-30-06

IF the **New York Times** reviews it at all, they'll only talk about the Ann Coulter action-figure doll, so I think I'll write my own review:

> **Godless** begins with a murder at the Louvre and then takes readers on a roller-coaster ride through the Church of Liberalism in a desperate game of cat and mouse in which the hunter becomes the hunted—with a twist at the end you simply won't believe! It's a real page-turner—even the book-on-tape version and large-print edition! Who knew a book about politics could make such an ideal gift—especially with Father's Day just two weeks away!
> —"My Review of My Book," 6-8-06

Q: How many liberals do you think there actually are in this country?

A: Way too many, but that's just a rough estimate. You know, somewhere in the ballpark of "way too many."
—"Top Secret Interview Exposed!," 7-5-06

Q: What is it that you would say inspires you?

A: Love of God and country.

Q: Why do you think you do what you do?

A: Love of God and country (and it's a great gig).
—Interview, FrontPage Magazine, 1-12-04

I NOTE that many are interested in my next [book] advance, so let me take this opportunity to point out that I have sold hundreds of thousands of copies of each of the three books I have written. My advance is based on performance. Liberal authors get big advances when they don't sell. —Interview, *Insight* magazine, 9-16-03

[Last time Ann cried]
TEARS of joy, when Clinton was impeached. —Interview, *New York Observer,* 8-20-02

THERE'S a joke about a Frenchman, an Englishman, and a Russian who are told they have only one day until the end of the world. The Frenchman says he will spend his last day with a bottle of Bordeaux and a beautiful woman. The Englishman says he will take his favorite sheepdog for a walk across the moors. The Russian says he will burn down his neighbor's house. I'm with the Russian. —"I'd Burn My Neighbor's House Down," 9-15-00

Q: Entre nous, what's the new book about? When will it be finished and available?
A: I was going to tell you, but then you started with that **entre nous** business. You know how I hate anything French. —Interview, NewsMax, 9-28-05

Q: Is there an evangelical leader like [Jerry] Falwell you most identify with?

A: I prefer a real Bible scholar—like, say, Howard Dean.
—Interview, NewsMax, 7-06

THAT'S the strange thing about liberal attacks on me: They can't hide me from the public. People can see me talking on TV, they can read my columns. Liberals aren't going to be able to persuade people that I'm giving orders to Salvadoran death squads.
—Interview, *New York Observer*, 8-25-03

I'M exposing liberal ideology for the pack of lies it is. What people do with that information is up to them, although one would hope it might come in handy on Election Day. —Interview, *Baltimore Sun*, 7-30-06

IF what I say is so outrageous, why don't they quote me accurately? —*The Matt Drudge Show*, 6-11-06

I LIKE to appear on the cover of my books in cocktail dresses, smiling, because it appears to enrage liberals when I do that.
—Interview, AOL's Book Maven, 9-17-06

WHO would you rather live under, me or Hillary Clinton? I wouldn't tell you you couldn't enjoy a little tobacco pleasure at a bar. —Interview, Salon, 7-25-03

EVERY liberal book being written right now is merely a response to **Slander**—[Joe] Conason, [David] Brock, [Al] Franken. **Treason** is going to keep them tied up for the next thirty years. —Interview, *New York Observer*, 8-25-03

Q: Have you ever thought of running for elected office?

A: No, but if I did, I'd run for the U.S. Senate from New York. Those people will elect just about anybody!
—Interview, *The Jewish Press*, 7-4-06

LIBERALS hate me because I understand them better than they understand themselves. —Interview, *The New York Observer*, 6-11-06

I WROTE a book, and liberals were hysterical. It's getting to be kind of kabuki theater. I write a book, they're hysterical. It happens all the time. —*Tonight Show with Jay Leno*, 6-14-06

LENO: See, my thing is, it's sort of more flies with honey. You make your point even if you get a couple of digs in, you make your point . . .

COULTER: I'm not really trying to attract people. If I wanted to attract people, you know, I'd wear sexy dresses, grow my hair long.

—*Tonight Show with Jay Leno*, 6-14-06

I REALLY like Deadheads and the whole Dead concert scene: the tailgating, the tie-dye uniforms, the camaraderie—it was like NASCAR for potheads. —Interview, Jambands, 6-23-06

Q: What do you enjoy most about your life as a bestselling author and columnist? . . .

A: Enjoy most: the prospect of having an impact on the public debate. Irritating liberals is a close second.

—Interview, *Human Events*, 6-6-06

TAUNTING liberals is like having a pet that does tricks. **Sit! Beg! Shake!** Then they do it. —Interview, *New York Observer*, 8-20-02

[**THE** media misquoting me] happens so much, I don't even keep track of it anymore. The last one I remember was when I said, "Cutting the tax rate on capital gains seems to have increased tax receipts for fiscal 2006, just as supply-side economics predicted it would." It came out in the paper as "I worship Adolf Hitler and share all of his goals, especially the 'final solution' to the 'Jewish problem.'" I have no idea how it happens, given the strict objectivity and rigid nonpartisanship of the American media. —Interview, *Baltimore Sun*, published in "What I Did on My Summer Vacation," 8-2-06

I'M still waiting for my detractors of any stripe to identify the inaccuracies in my book that would lead them to conclude that I went "overboard." However, I am no longer holding my breath. —Interview, FrontPage Magazine, 12-23-03

Q: Your book is entitled **How to Talk to a Liberal (If You Must)**. Let's back up a step: How do you recognize that the person standing in front of you is a liberal in the first place?

A: I can usually tell by the corduroy jacket.
—Interview, Citizenlink, 10-19-04

[On liberals' fake documentary that shows Bush being assassinated]

HENCEFORTH I think we can dispense with "Mean Ann Coulter." —*Hannity & Colmes*, 8-31-06

I'M here, I'm not queer, and I'm not going away. —*Lou Dobbs Tonight*, 6-8-06

I HATE talking about Ann Coulter. . . . I'm not important, what I talk about is important. —*The Big Idea with Donny Deutsch*, 11-2-06

AS far as I'm concerned, I'm a middle-of-the-road moderate and the rest of you are crazy. —"I'd Burn My Neighbor's House Down," 9-15-00

Q: Are you a neoconservative?
A: No, I'm a gentile.
—Interview, *New York Observer*, 4-29-03

Q: So what are you?
A: Just your typical, immodest-dressing, swarthy male-loving, friend-to-homosexuals ultraconservative.
—Interview, *The Guardian* (U.K.), 5-17-03

CRIME AND PUNISHMENT: PREFERABLY A TWO-STEP PROCESS

The Democratic base is constantly in a state of indignation about the fact that criminals often end up in prison. It's as if the sixties, seventies, and eighties never happened. No matter how spectacular the failure of liberal crime policies in the past, the Democratic Party base has plans to overhaul the criminal justice system as soon as they get back into power. Beware: These people have a "To Do" list. Right after making sure abortions are legal up to the fortieth trimester, they plan to empty the prisons so liberal busybodies can start addressing the "root causes" of crime. Though it has never worked in the past, liberals believe we must understand criminals in order to address the problem of crime.

In other areas, understanding motives is not so important to liberals. How about the Holocaust? What made this Hitler guy tick, I wonder? What motivated him? You don't just kill six million Jews for no reason.

And if understanding a criminal's motive is so important, why aren't we told **exactly** what the rape victim was wearing? Wouldn't that go a long way to helping us understand the rapist's motive? How about attacks on gays? Maybe gay-bashers are just tired of being told they have no sense of style. You know how sarcastic gay guys can be. Only in the case of violent criminals (other than un-PC criminals) are liberals driven by this weird obsession of understanding the perpetrators' motive.

I don't recall any liberals wanting to understand Enron CEO Ken Lay. They held candlelight vigils for Ted Bundy and Tookie Williams but rejoiced when Ken Lay died. If only we could get liberals to hate child-molesters and cop-killers as much as they hate Ken Lay, we might be able to trust them with crime policy. Maybe we could get liberals to support the death penalty by telling them it's only for white-collar criminals. Liberals believe no punishment is too unusual or too cruel for rich guys engaged in insider trading. I think it's cruel and unusual to have to listen to sanctimonious B-list Hollywood actors tell us how compassionate they are for opposing the death penalty. Surely we can all agree: That's too cruel even for Ken Lay.

IF the death penalty doesn't deter murder, how come Michael Moore is still alive and I'm not on death row? —*Godless*, **pp. 25-26**

CRIMINALS and poor people allow [liberals] to swell with a sense of their own incredible self-worth. That's the whole point of being a liberal: to feel superior to people with less money. —*Slander*, **p. 29**

[**LBJ**'s Attorney General Ramsey] Clark believed it was the government's job to rehabilitate violent criminals, not to keep them away from the public. "Prisons," Clark said, "are usually little more than places to keep people." Yes—I think that's the idea in a nutshell. —*Godless*, p. 35

[LIBERALS complain that] we're the only modern democracy with the death penalty. I think that should be treated as a selling point: "Come to the United States for the economic opportunity, stay because we fry our Ted Bundys!"—*Godless*, p. 25

THE proposition that prison doesn't work is like saying deodorant doesn't work (which college liberals also seem to believe). Of course prison works: It keeps people who commit crimes off the streets because they're in prison. Let's run the numbers: The recidivism rate of armed robbers behind bars is . . . hmmmm, looks like 0 percent! —*Godless*, p. 43

[LIBERALS] have an irreducible fascination with barbarism and will defend anything hateful—Tookie, Mumia, Saddam Hussein, Hedda Nussbaum, abortion, the North American Man/Boy Love Association, **New York Times** columnist Frank Rich. —*Godless*, p. 10

I LIKE how all the same criminal defense attorneys go from defending O.J. to defending Clinton to defending Saddam Hussein. —*Hannity & Colmes*, 7-1-04

NEEDLESS to say, the death penalty is always verboten, except in the narrow case of Enron executives or clothing designers who use fur. —*Godless*, p. 24

THE only cop the **New York Times** likes is the one in the Village People. —"They Weren't Overzealous This Time," 6-19-00

DEAR ANN: FREE ADVICE WORTH EVERY PENNY

I am in no way even remotely qualified to be giving anyone any sort of advice on any subject. Which is to say I am every bit as qualified to dispense free advice as Dear Abby, Ann Landers, Dr. Joyce Brothers, Dr. Phil, and every other published advice columnist I have ever read. Plus, all of my advice on how to deal with liberals is battle-tested and guaranteed to work. There is less advice here than in **Poor Richard's Almanack,** but what makes my advice better is that you will find absolutely nothing about rising early.

HERE'S a foolproof method for keeping America safe: Always do the exact 180-degree opposite of whatever Jimmy Carter says as quickly as possible.
—*"Guantánamo Loses Five-Star Rating,"* 6-22-05

IF you are not being called outrageous by liberals, you're not being outrageous enough. —*How to Talk to a Liberal (If You Must),* p. 10

WE don't have to adopt all the Democrats' traits—incessant lying, utter shamelessness, criminal behavior, and lots of crying—but Republicans need to tattoo this truism on their arms: It's never a good idea to take advice from your enemies. —*"It's Never a Good Idea to Take Advice from Your Enemies,"* 7-21-04

HISTORICALLY, the best way to convert liberals is to have them move out of their parents' home, get a job, and start paying taxes. —*How to Talk to a Liberal (If You Must),* p. 1

[Advice to high school Republican]
GET your parents to buy you my books, my books on tape, my action figure, and the soon-to-be-released Ann Coulter abstinence kit (which is an 8 × 10 glossy of Susan Estrich), important for boys your age. —YAF Questions from Students, 1-07

[**M**]**Y** philosophy on arguing with liberals is: Tough love, except I don't love them. In most cases I don't even like them. In other words, my "tough love" approach is much like the Democrats' "middle-class tax cuts"—everything but the last word. —*How to Talk to a Liberal (If You Must)*, p. 17

Q: Your last book is called: **How to Talk to a Liberal.** With which words?
A: A baseball bat is best. But if you absolutely must use words, something like: "Grow up."
—Interview, *Il Foglio* (Italy), 10-04

YOU know you're doing something right when you've reduced hordes of liberals to blind, sputtering rage. —Interview, *Human Events*, 6-29-06

DEMOCRAT IDEAS
(SEE ALSO: MARX, LENIN)

In general, I'm against big government, but I would support a massive emergency federal program to teach logic to liberals.

In lieu of rational argument, liberals refer to the beliefs of "Americans," "the vast majority," "all men of goodwill"—and then cite an utterly implausible source for the beliefs of Americans, like professional former Republican Kevin Phillips. They simply utter these ringing Augustinian farts, which there is absolutely no reason to believe are true. On the basis of what scientific survey have the editors of the **New York Times** determined the beliefs of the "vast majority"? As I recall, Pauline Kael, theater critic for **The New Yorker,** blithely expressed the sentiments of her journalist peers when she wondered how Nixon could have won a landslide election in 1972, since no one she knew voted for him.

Democrat ideas tend to have the most support before anyone has had time to think about them. Gun-control laws have only become less popular the more people have thought about them. The federal income tax has not gained in popularity since it was introduced in 1913. Abortion has not become more acceptable since 1970. The belief in global warming has declined steadily since its zenith, which was back before anyone knew what it was. The more people learn about Democrat ideas, the more they hate them. This is a corollary to the rule that people are always conservative in their own areas of expertise.

This is the danger with allowing Democrats to have ideas in the first place. It is possible that at some brief moment in time, a "vast majority" will agree with liberals—as with embryonic stem-cell research, provided one defines "vast majority" as "bare plurality" or "everyone Paul Krugman knows personally." As Trotsky said, people with no politics develop the worst possible politics at the worst time.

LIBERALS have been wrong about everything in the last half-century.

They were wrong about Stalin (praised in the **New York Times** and known as "Uncle Joe" to Franklin Roosevelt). They were wrong about Reagan (won the Cold War and now polling as the greatest president of the twentieth century). They were wrong about the Soviet Union (defeated by the twentieth century's greatest president). They were wrong even about their precious "Abraham Lincoln Brigade" in the Spanish Civil War (the disgorging of Soviet archives proves that the Lincoln Brigade was part of "a rigidly controlled Soviet operation"). They were wrong about Nicaragua (Communist dictatorships in Latin America turned out not to be "inevitable revolutions" after all). They were wrong about welfare (since overhauled by Republicans to notable success). They were wrong about crime (Giuliani's achievement is evident in the number of candidates who promise to continue his policies). They were wrong about Social Security (now heading toward bankruptcy). They were wrong about the Civil Rights Act (which was never going to be used as an instrument of discrimination against whites). They were wrong on the sexual revolution (witness the explosions of AIDS, herpes, chlamydia, hepatitis B, and abortion).

It is not an accident that, today, the Left's single biggest cause is "global warming." This time, conservatives won't be able to prove them wrong for a thousand years. —*Slander,* p. 197

LIBERALS are always complaining that they haven't figured out how to distill their message to slogans and bumper stickers— as they allege Republicans have. Though it can't be easy to fit the entire **Communist Manifesto** on a bumper sticker, I beg to differ. (Bumper sticker version of the current Democratic platform: "Ask me about how I'm going to raise your taxes.") —**The 'Mainstream' Is Located in France,"** 10-30-03

DEMOCRATS are terrific at building alliances. Remember how Jimmy Carter won the love of the world by ditching our ally the shah of Iran, allowing him to be replaced by a string of crazy ayatollahs? Since then, we haven't heard a peep from that area of the world. —*"C'est Si Bon,"* 5-9-07

[**A HOWARD** Dean campaign worker said] that she was first attracted to Dean based on his policy of having a state social worker visit every new mother in Vermont (not to be confused with the Arkansas policy from the 1980s in which the governor would visit every woman who was hoping to become pregnant). Not that I'm trying to privatize anything here, but in my home state of Connecticut, a new mother is traditionally visited by her own mother. —**"Vegan Computer Geeks for Dean,"** 12-12-03

LIBERALS don't read books—they don't read anything. That's why they're liberals. They watch TV, absorb the propaganda, and vote on the basis of urges. —**Interview, NewsMax,** 7-02

LIBERALS have been completely intellectually vanquished. Actually, they lost the war of ideas long ago. It's just that now their defeat is so obvious, even they've noticed. —"Come Back, Liberals!," 3-9-05

IT is the Democrats who have turned the Confederate flag into a federal issue, because they relish nothing more than being morally indignant. Not about abortion, adultery, illegitimacy, the divorce rate, or a president molesting an intern and lying to federal investigators. . . . Democrats stake out a clear moral position only on the issue of slavery. Of course, when it mattered, they were on the wrong side of that issue, too. —*How to Talk to a Liberal (If You Must)*, p. 171

I'M rooting for the faction of the Democratic Party [like Nancy Pelosi] . . . taking the position that our ideas are fine. **That's right, class, do not change anything about what we believe. We've just got to package the wine in new bottles. We need a new way of delivering our message, but the message**

is perfect! We just need to advertise RU-486 at NASCAR or something—that'll do the trick! I think the trick is, they need to obfuscate their message. —Interview, *New York Observer,* 1-10-05

[E]VERY time the government tries to help the poor it ends up removing the marvelous incentives life provides to do things like buy an alarm clock, get a job, keep your knees together before marriage, and generally become a productive, happy member of society. —"Bush's Compassionate Conservatism," 8-29-00

[S]UPPORT for all liberal ideas is always at its zenith before people figure out what liberals are talking about. (This is known as "the Howard Dean effect.") —*Godless,* p. 91

NEVER mind trusting liberals with national security. Never mind trusting them with raising kids. These people shouldn't even be allowed to own pets. —"Are Videotaped Beheadings Covered by Geneva?," 9-20-06

[T]HE essence of being a liberal: the absolute conviction that there is one set of rules for you and another, completely different set of rules for everyone else. —*How to Talk to a Liberal (If You Must)*, pp. 279-80

DEMOCRATS' VIRTUES: POINTS OF LIGHT IN A SEA OF DARKNESS

You always hear people say conservatives see the world only in black-and-white, lacking the ability to see the other fellow's point of view (unlike, say, the flexible Hillary Clinton). The following quotes prove that I am perfectly able to recognize Democrats' good points.

THE good part of being a Democrat is that you can commit crimes, sell out your base, bomb foreigners, and rape a woman, and the Democratic faithful will still think you're the greatest. —*Slander,* p. 157

THIS is liberalism's real strength. It is no longer susceptible to **reductio ad absurdum** arguments. Before you can come up with a comical take on their worldview, some college professor has already written an article advancing the idea.—*Godless*, p. 280

Q: Tell us how you regard President Franklin Roosevelt. What, if anything, do you admire most about him?

A: I admire that he smoked in public and he did not insist on getting approval from France and Germany before going to war.
—Interview, American Enterprise Institute, 2004

ELECTIONS: IT ONLY ENCOURAGES THEM

In my lifetime, presidential elections have consisted not so much of Democrats versus Republicans, or even liberals versus conservatives, but the Straitjacket Party versus the Sane Party.

In the seventies and eighties, the Democratic Party decided to re-create itself by getting rid of all the normal people.

Get rid of that guy—the head of the auto union. He's antichoice!

Really? Do we have to? He's been a member of the Democratic Party for eighteen years.

Yeah, well, maybe now we can hear from the *REST* of America!

John Kerry was the most left-wing person the Democrats had ever nominated for president, but because today's Democrats are crazy, they thought Kerry was the safe, middle-of-the-road choice. He had a war record! Not only that, but most of his war record was captured on eight-millimeter films Kerry made in a war zone. Although Kerry served in Vietnam, what really launched his career as a Democrat was his rather more provocative service as an antiwar military veteran accusing his comrades of being murderers, rapists, and war criminals.

Only the Democrats could think they would bolster their national security credentials by nominating the most hated Vietnam veteran in America for president. Out of seventy million registered Democrats, a guy who helped run the Winter Soldier hearings was their pick. (But to be fair, out of their seventy million members, only six were veterans.)

When Kerry lost and Bush won, the **New York Times** expressed the wide diversity of opinion about the election on its op-ed page with a column by Garry Wills saying that Bush won because of a fundamentalist Christian "jihad" and with a column by Maureen Dowd saying Bush's victory was the result of a fundamentalist Christian "jihad." (By the way, if Dowd's candidate had won, she'd be being fitted for a burka about now.) Rounding out the Left's explanation for failure was Michael Moore, who began ridiculing the vast expanse of "red states" as "Jesusland." Ironically, some Democrats were so despondent they even contemplated—hushed whisper—prayer.

When they win, they won. When we win, we cheated. This philosophy has served the Democratic Party well since 1976, the last time the Democrats got a majority of Americans to vote for them (1976, Jimmy Carter, with a decisive 50.1 percent of the vote).

Q: Who will win the elections in 2004?
A: That's for the Supreme Court to sort out, you ignorant foreigner.
—Interview, *Il Foglio* (Italy), 10-04

I LOVE these jackasses [in Florida in the 2000 election] claiming they meant to vote for Gore but—whoops!—slipped and pulled the lever for Buchanan instead! Oh really. Let's pretend that's true. Sorry, but that's one of the disabilities of being a political party that preys on the stupid. Sometimes your "base" forgets it's Election Day, too. Live by demagoguing to the feeble-minded, die by demagoguing to the feeble-minded. —"Just Go!," 11-9-00

THE protesters [at the Republican National Convention] have been kind of pathetic this week, don't you think? A **hundred thousand**? You can get a hundred thousand if you put five Dominican girls in bikinis. —Interview, *New York Observer*, 9-13-04

[**IN** 2004] Democrats tried explaining that they were being shellacked by the superior media savvy and rhetorical skills of Republicans—like that silver-tongued devil George Bush. . . . They said they just needed to retool their message, formulate winning sound bites, and talk about "God's green earth," and maybe Democrats wouldn't keep frightening people. But the retooling didn't work. It turned out it really was the message that Americans hated. —*Godless*, pp. 100-101

MY pick [for president] so far is the guy in Philly who put up the "this is America—please order in English" sign in his sandwich shop. Hey, at least the guy has a coherent immigration policy. —Interview, *Baltimore Sun*, 7-30-06

THE swing voters—I like to refer to them as the idiot voters because they don't have set philosophical principles. You're either a liberal or you're a conservative if you have an IQ above a toaster. —Interview, *Beyond the News*, 6-4-00

WAY too many people vote. We should have fewer people voting. There ought to be a poll tax to take the literacy test before voting. —*Your World with Neil Cavuto*, 9-29-06

Q: Who exactly has the vote who shouldn't have?
A: Women. It's true. It would be a much better country if women did not vote. That is simply a fact. In fact, in every

presidential election since 1950—except Goldwater in '64—the Republican would have won, if only the men had voted.
—Interview, *The Guardian* (U.K.), 5-17-03

THE common wisdom holds that "both parties" have to appeal to the extremes during the primary and then move to the center for the general election. To the contrary, both parties run for office as conservatives. Once they have fooled the voters and are safely in office, Republicans sometimes double-cross the voters. Democrats always do. —**"Massachusetts Supreme Court Abolishes Capitalism," 11-27-03**

BUSH won the largest popular vote in history with a 3.5 million margin. Indeed, simply by getting a majority of the country to vote for him, the Left's most hated politician since Richard Nixon, Bush did something "rock star" Bill Clinton never did. —**"One Last Flip-Flop," 11-3-04**

IF I were a Democrat, I wouldn't have an opinion on [our presidential nominees].

I'd wait until one candidate emerged from the pack as a front-runner, then pretend I'd been supporting that candidate all along, like the sniveling, gutless little America-hater I would be if I were a Democrat.
—Interview, *Baltimore Sun*, 7-30-06

ENVIRONMENTALISM: ADOLF HITLER WAS THE FIRST ENVIRONMENTALIST

Read this chapter immediately! Global warming is going to result in a big ice storm tomorrow, and we're all going to have to hide with Maggie Gyllenhaal's little brother in the New York Public Library.

Oh wait—here's another idea: How about our great-grandkids get their own planet?

THE temperature of the planet has increased about one degree Fahrenheit in the last century. So imagine a summer afternoon when it's 63 degrees and the next thing you know it's . . . 64 degrees. Ahhhhhhhhhhhhhh!!!!!!!!!! Run for your lives, everybody! Women and children first! Help! Where's FEMA, dammit? —Interview, *Right Wing News*, 6-16-06

LIBERALS don't care about the environment. The core of environmentalism is a hatred for mankind. They want mass infanticide, zero population growth, reduced standards of living, and vegetarianism. Most crucially, they want Americans to stop with their infernal deodorant use. —"Global Warming: The French Connection," 5-29-03

LIBERAL environmentalists admire the living situation of the earthworm and believe humans should emulate it. —CNS News, 6-6-06

ENVIRONMENTALISTS' energy plan is the repudiation of America and Christian destiny, which is Jet Skis, steak on the electric grill, hot showers, and night skiing. —*Godless*, p. 7

IN the 1970s, Paul Ehrlich wrote the best-selling book **The Population Bomb**, predicting a global famine and warning that entire nations would cease to exist by the end of the twentieth century—among them England. . . . In 2001—despite the perplexing persistent existence of England—the Sierra Club listed Ehrlich's **Population Bomb** as among its books recommended by Sierra readers. How many trees had to be chopped down to make the paper for all those copies of **The Population Bomb?** —*Godless*, p. 8

A SPARROW does not a spring make, but in the Druid religion of environmentalism, every warm summer's breeze prompts apocalyptic demands for a ban on aerosol spray and plastic bags. —*Godless*, p. 188

[L]IBERALS are never sorry to rid the world of what they—like Goebbels—view as "useless eaters" in order to improve the parking situation in Santa Monica. —Interview, NewsMax, 7-06

GOD gave us the earth. We have dominion over the plants, the animals, the trees. God said, "Earth is yours. Take it. Rape it. It's yours." —*Hannity & Colmes*, 6-20-01

IT'S wacky enough for liberals to believe in global warming—but that we would run out of natural resources? It rains. The water doesn't go away. And now because of liberal government bureaucrats who decided that we can only have two table-spoons of water in the toilet, you throw half a tissue in the toilet and you have to flush it sixteen times. —**Interview, Salon,** 7-25-03

GLOBAL warming enthusiasts use "the weather" the way Soviet dictators did (and as do bureaucrats in a closely related field, the airlines). Irrespective of what the weather conditions are, "the weather" supports their point that fifty years of bad harvests aren't the fault of central planning (and that we can't take off for another six hours). —**"Our Mistake—Keep Polluting,"** 9-8-00

LIBERALS want us to live like Swedes, with their genial, mediocre lives, ratcheting back our expectations, practicing fuel austerity, and sitting by the fire in a cardigan sweater like Jimmy Carter. —*Godless,* p. 6

IN 2004, former vice president Al Gore gave a speech on global warming in New York City on the coldest day of the year. Warm trends prove global warming. Cold trends also prove global warming. This is the philosophy of a madman. —*Godless,* p. 190

MY ideal America would have no liberals and seven-gallon flush toilets in every bathroom. —Interview, *Baltimore Sun,* 7-30-06

EVOLUTION, ALCHEMY, AND OTHER "SETTLED" SCIENTIFIC THEORIES

The only person more popular than Charles Darwin at this point is B. Hussein Obama. This beady-eyed fly-torturer (Darwin, not Obama, but keep your eye on him, too) gave us a conclusionary theory that has become a crucial part of how we are programmed to think in nonspiritual terms.

The Left's neurotic obsession with Darwinism is more than their usual illiterate disdain for any intelligence in the universe other than themselves. This is the linchpin of their man-based religion, designed to poison young minds from the beginning. The road from Darwinism to Nazism may not be ineluctable, but it's more ineluctable than the progress of monkey to man.

For all the fascinating theories the Darwiniacs have spun, they still have nothing in the way of actual evidence for their theory. They simply believe the evidence is there, just as they believed the evidence wasn't there on the Rosenbergs. Their groundbreaking discoveries "proving" Darwinism turned out to be colossal hoaxes concocted by people hoping to win a Nobel Prize. I've seen more compelling scientific theories under the byline "Uncle Remus."

The theory of evolution shouldn't be taught as fact, although I don't have a problem with it being sung around campfires at summer camps alongside other popular fables and legends.

LIBERALS' creation myth is Charles Darwin's theory of evolution, which is about one notch above Scientology in scientific rigor. —*Godless*, p. 199

FAR from chastely refusing to acknowledge miracles, evolutionists are the primary source of them. These aren't chalk-covered scientists toiling away with their test tubes and Bunsen burners. They are religious fanatics for whom evolution must be true and any evidence to the contrary—including, for example, the entire fossil record—is something that must be explained away with a fanciful excuse, like "Our evidence didn't fossilize." —*Godless*, pp. 244-45

NO matter what argument you make against evolution, the response is **Well, you know it's possible to believe in evolution and believe in God.** Yes, and it's possible to believe in Spiderman and believe in God, but that doesn't prove Spiderman is true. —*Godless*, p. 246

THE Darwinists have saved the sanctity of their temples: the public schools. They didn't win on science, persuasion, or the evidence. They won the way liberals always win: by finding a court to hand them everything they want on a silver platter. —*Godless*, p. 200

IF only Darwinism were true, someday we might evolve public schools with the ability to entertain opposable ideas about the creation of man. —"Hey You, Browsing *Godless*—Buy the Book or Get Out!," 6-7-06

MUCH like George Bush's alleged draft dodging, there are only two possible answers from the Darwiniacs: Either evolution is true or more research is needed. —*Godless*, p. 226

THE Darwin cult has the audacity to compare the theory of evolution to Einstein's theory of relativity, saying it is "just a theory," too. Okay, but when Einstein announced his theory of general relativity, he also offered a series of empirical tests that would prove it false. . . . By contrast, Darwin imagined a mechanism that accounts for how life in its infinite variety might have arisen and offered a nondisprovable standard to test his theory. —*Godless*, p. 242

FROM beginning to end, the Scopes trial was a scheme cooked up in New York and pawned off on the good citizens of Dayton

[Tennessee], much like **Cats.** —*Godless,* p. 259

[T]HE only thing that can be said for certain about Darwinism is that it would take less time for (1) a single-celled organism to evolve into a human being through mutation and natural selection than for (2) Darwinists to admit they have no proof of (1). —"Hey You, Browsing *Godless*—Buy the Book or Get Out!," 6-7-06

FOREIGNERS, OR THE "NON-SOAP-ORIENTED"

They're no good. Don't trust 'em—except Denmark, Australia, the Czech Republic, and the rest of new Europe, which, amazingly enough, has recently come to include France and Germany. Maybe foreigners aren't so bad as long as Bush is president. Canadians, for example, are either great or awful, and at the outset of the War on Terror, the balance was swinging perilously close to awful. Better shape up, Canada! At this point, we're only keeping you around for the beer.

Q: Why do Europeans prefer liberals to conservatives?

A: Because you're all a bunch of atheists, humanists, and moral relativists. Love the food, though! And don't get me started on the shoes you wonderful people make! They're to surrender for!
—Interview, *Il Foglio* (Italy), 10-04

DID you see that the Sri Lankans would not accept medical teams from Israel [after the tsunami]? "It's a natural disaster, we're dying, send help! No Jews." O-kay. Lovely people.—Interview, *New York Observer*, 1-10-05

AMERICANS were solidly behind the president in fighting terrorism, so liberals went and sulked with their cheese-tasting friends. —*Treason*, p. 218

THE very idea of foreigners voting on America's national security is absurd. How about getting them to vote on the country's smoking policies? —*Treason*, p. 218

WE must attack France. What are they going to do? Fight us? —"Attack France!," 12-20-01

I THINK we ought to nuke North Korea right now just to give the rest of the world a warning . . . POW! —Interview, *New York Observer*, 1-10-05

Q: What is your opinion about the center-left leader in Europe? Zapatero, Blair, Schröder?

A: Zapatero is Spanish for "Chamberlain." I would campaign for Blair for U.S. president.
Schröder—what is the Italian word for "scumbag"?

Q: And about center-right? Berlusconi, Chirac?

A: Chirac is center-right? Better lay off the grappa, Primo.
Berlusconi: **Love** him!!
—Interview, *Il Foglio* (Italy), 10-04

IF this country didn't have the stomach to stand up for its principles, we'd be Canada

by now. —*High Crimes and Misdemeanors,*
p. 20

IT'S always, I might add, the worst Americans who end up going [to Canada]. The
Tories after the Revolutionary War, the
Vietnam draft dodgers after Vietnam. And
now after this election, you have the blue-
state people moving up there. —*Hannity &
Colmes,* 11-30-04

COULTER: [Canada] need[s] us. They
better hope the United States doesn't roll
over one night and crush them. They are
lucky we allow them to exist on the same
continent. . . .

COLMES: Ann, thank you for allowing
me to exist in the same planet as you. I
appreciate it.

COULTER: You're welcome.
—*Hannity & Colmes,* 11-30-04

PUBLIC opinion in Europe was strongly
against the United States [going to war with
Iraq]. Of course, public opinion in Europe
was also for pogroms. —*Treason,* p. 218

GAYS: NO GAY LEFT BEHIND!

The media love describing the Republican Party base as "antigay"—as opposed to "anti-gay marriage." If they thought they could get away with it, they'd call Republicans "anti-civil rights."

Let's see who's antigay. Gays are the victims of hate crimes, or as Republicans call them, "crimes." In the gay enclave of West Hollywood law and order prevail: Every lawn is fastidiously manicured, there is no trash, cops are everywhere, and the average "Parking Restrictions" sign is longer than **Gone With the Wind.** Gays have high incomes— a study a few years ago says 60 percent higher than the median income in America. In Islamic countries, gays are punished with death. Consequently, the three most important issues for any sane gay person ought to be crime, taxes, and the war on Islamic fascists.

The Democratic Party supports criminals and Islamic terrorists but has no sympathy for taxpayers. To the contrary, they perennially want to raise taxes—or as they say, "invest in our future." But this future we're always "investing" in does not seem to include any gay people. Democrats love using the tax code to enact lots of special-interest goodies with great appeal to suburban soccer moms but of absolutely no use to most gays, such as child tax credits, tuition tax credits, child-care credits, education savings accounts, student loans, the Family and Medical Leave Act, and the "Please Vote for Me, Soccer Mom!" Act. There is only one issue more important to the Democrats than raising taxes and that is keeping abortion legal at all stages of pregnancy. This is probably not a big issue for most gays.

After surrendering to Muslim terrorists and common criminals, aborting babies, and raising taxes, the Left's favorite pastime is outing gay Republicans. Liberals claim to love gays, but their default comeback to a conservative they disagree with is to call him gay. It's gotten to the point that we need a Nasdaq ticker just to know what the Democratic Party's current position on gays is. Even Chris Rock is said to be offended by this level of gay-bashing. Liberals insist on letting gay men lead Boy Scouts on overnight camping trips, but won't let a gay man be a Republican.

Manifestly, Republican policies are more pro-gay than Democrat policies and we don't make a sport of outing political opponents who happen to be gay. We just don't like gay marriage. The purpose of marriage is not to sanctify the intense feelings people have for each other. The purpose is to harness men's predatory biological impulses into a paired heterosexual relationship directed toward raising children. Mankind has never concocted a better scheme for civilizing men than marriage. And while we're on the subject, animalkind has never developed a better mechanism for destroying civilization than liberalism.

174

[I]F you think that Christianity is tough on homosexuality, you should hear what your pals, the Muslims, do to them. —Interview, *The Guardian* (U.K.), 5-17-03

I LIKE gays. I like all gays, and not just the ones who are Ann Coulter drag queens. —*Kudlow & Company,* 7-28-06

WE need to get a rule book from the Democrats [on gays]:

- Boy Scouts: As gay as you want to be.
- Priests: No gays!
- Democratic politicians: Proud gay Americans.
- Republican politicians: Presumed guilty.
- White House press corps: No gays, unless they hate Bush.
- Active-duty U.S. military: As gay as possible.
- Men who date Liza Minnelli: Do I have to draw you a picture, Miss Thing?

—"Who Knew Congressman Foley Was a Closeted Democrat?," 10-4-06

YOU would think there were "Straights Only" water fountains the way Democrats carry on so (as if any gay man would drink nonbottled water). —**"Massachusetts Supreme Court Abolishes Capitalism," 11-27-03**

THOUSANDS of gay men died and their blood is on the hands of the so-called AIDS activists who thought it was more important to push their political and social agendas than it was to educate gay men about the dangers of public, anonymous, promiscuous, multiple-partner unprotected sex. Or, as it's known in West Hollywood, "Friday night." —**Interview,** *Right Wing News,* **6-16-06**

SPEAKING of gay marriage, as long as liberals are so big on discussing "mandates" and whether Bush has one (they say he does not), I think the one thing we can all agree on is that there is definitely a "mandate" against gay marriage. In fact, a clear majority of us are uncomfortable with the word "mandate" because it sounds like Wayne asking Stephen out for dinner and a movie. —"**The Loss That Keeps On Giving!**," 11-17-04

I HATE having this argument [about sodomy laws] foisted on me by the Supreme Court. Part of what democracy allows you to do is to not give a damn about some issues. —Interview, Salon, 7-25-03

[**On** Brokeback Mountain]
IS the idea of gay cowboys really that new? Didn't the Village People do that a couple of decades ago? Am I the only person who saw John Travolta in **Urban Cowboy**?

Movies with the same groundbreaking theme to come:

- **Westward Homo!**
- **The Magnificent, Fabulous Seven**
- **Gunfight at the K-Y Corral**
- **How West Hollywood Was Won**

—"Speaking Truth to Dead Horses: My Oscar Predictions," 3-1-06

Q: Let's say you had to stay home and watch reruns of either **Sex and the City**

or **Friends.** Which program would you select and why?

A: **Friends.** Because I'm not a gay male.
—Interview, American Enterprise Institute, 2004

[O]UR gays are more macho than their straights. —"Calling the Kettle Gay," 3-2-05

THE big argument for "civil unions"—but not marriage!—is that gays are denied ordinary civil rights here in the American Taliban. This is where gays usually bring up the argument about all the straight couples living in "sham" marriages, but I see no point in dragging the Clintons into this.
—"Massachusetts Supreme Court Abolishes Capitalism," 11-27-03

[L]IBERALS say: "We love gay people! Gay people are awesome! Being gay is awesome! Gay marriage is awesome! Gay cartoon characters are awesome! And if you don't agree with us we'll punish you by telling everyone that you're gay!"—"Calling the Kettle Gay," 3-2-05

THIS is a perfect example of the Democrats way overplaying their hands. They're talking about, you know, just because [Congressman Mark] Foley is gay and sending e-mails asking a kid what he wants for his birthday, we should have been wiretapping the guy's phone. They don't want to wiretap people getting calls from al Qaeda, but we're supposed to be wiretapping a guy because he's gay? —*The O'Reilly Factor,* 10-3-06

MATTHEWS: How do you know that Bill Clinton's gay?

COULTER: He may not be gay, but Al Gore—total fag.

—*Hardball with Chris Matthews,* 7-26-06

GIRLS: CHICKS HATE IT WHEN YOU CALL THEM "GIRLS"

Mercifully, the mewling soccer moms of elections past have faded into irrelevance. Gun-toting right-wing college coeds are ascendant. Soccer moms' entire political calculus boils down to how "we" divide up the pie in order to ensure an equitable distribution of resources based on their fantastical notions of how wealth originates. The pretty College Republican girls are more interested in asking: Who bakes the pie?

GIRL-POWER feminists who got where they are by marrying men with money or power—Hillary Clinton, Nancy Pelosi,

Arianna Huffington, and John Kerry—love to complain about how hard it is for a woman to be taken seriously. —"I Am Woman, Hear Me Bore," 1-24-07

FOR cocktails alone, I figure I owe the male population several thousand dollars. So I will be the one to step forward and say: To the extent one gender is oppressing the other, it's not women who should be complaining. —*How to Talk to a Liberal (If You Must)*, p. 327

COLMES: Hundreds of firefighters trained in search-and-rescue missions rushed to help the victims of Hurricane Katrina, but when some of these firefighters arrived at a FEMA center in Atlanta, the first task was a course on sexual harassment and equal opportunity employment. . . .

COULTER: I know. It's been on my web page for two weeks because I'm enraged at the idea that FEMA thinks any female would not want to be sexually harassed by a fireman.
—*Hannity & Colmes*, 9-27-05

[I]N a maniacal pursuit of equality . . . these querulous little feminists stripped women of the sense that they can rely on the institution of marriage and gave men license to discard their wives. But at least women can choose to be pigs now, too! This is what happens when you allow women to think about public policy. —"National Organization for Worms," 7-19-01

THERE'S a reason boys asking for dates is a convention of civilized society. Someone's going to have to face rejection. . . . Speaking for myself, I'll take 69 cents on the dollar (or whatever the current feminist myth is) never to have to ask for a date. —"Capital Punishment," 4-99

Q: What must the Republican Party do to appeal to more women?
A: Hmmm, I don't know. What **do** women want anyway?
—Interview, American Enterprise Institute, 2004

THAT was the theme of the Million Mom March: I don't need a brain—I've got a womb. —**"For Womb the Bell Tolls,"** 5-16-00

GUANTÁNAMO:
ROOM SERVICE, I'D LIKE
SEVENTY-TWO VIRGINS, PLEASE

Some terrorists being held at Guantánamo claimed they were tortured by being forced into uncomfortable, unnatural positions— sort of like the Democrats' position on abortion. But I say: If you have to live in Cuba, Guantánamo is the place to be! It's the Carnival Cruise line of prison camps! Not only do the terrorists have 600-thread-count sheets, but the chocolate-raspberry mousse sounds delicious. (I personally thought the gift shop T-shirts that said "My dad went to Guantánamo and all I got was this lousy T-shirt" went too far.) Needless to say, we pass out Korans to the little darlings to make sure they can stay up-to-date on their commitment to jihad. Giving Guantánamo detainees the Koran is like giving Jeffrey Dahmer **The Joy of Cooking.** Soon liberals will be recommending an audiobook version of the Koran read by Susan Sarandon for those who can't read but still want to hate the Jews.

IN the interests of helping my country, I have devised a compact set of torture guidelines for Guantánamo.

It's not torture if:

- The same acts performed on a live stage have been favorably reviewed by Frank Rich of the **New York Times**
- Andrew Sullivan has ever solicited it from total strangers on the Internet
- You can pay someone in New York to do it to you
- Karen Finley ever got a federal grant to do it
- It's comparable to the treatment U.S. troops received in basic training

• It's no worse than the way airlines treat little girls in pigtails flying to see Grandma.

—"Guantánamo Loses 5-Star Rating," 6-22-05

[O]NE recent menu for suspected terrorists at Guantánamo consisted of orange glazed chicken, fresh fruit crepe, steamed peas and mushrooms, and rice pilaf. Sounds like the sort of thing you'd get at Windows on the World—if it still existed. —"Guantánamo Loses 5-Star Rating," 6-22-05

THE Democratic base is at a fever pitch with visions of storm troopers listening to their phone calls and ruthlessly torturing innocent accountants at Guantánamo, where the average inmate has his own lawyer and his own prayer rug and is wondering what to do about that extra weight—known as the "Gitmo 20"—he's put on since being captured. —"Incoming Congress Prepares to Launch 'Operation Surrender,'" 12-6-06

THE Washington Post reported that a detainee at Guantánamo says he was "threatened with sexual abuse." (Bonus "Not Torture" rule: If it is similar to the way interns were treated in the Clinton White House.)

"Sign or you will be tortured!"

"What's the torture?"

"We will merely threaten you with horrible things!"

"That's it?"

"Shut up and do as we say, or we'll issue empty, laughable threats guaranteed to amuse you. This is your last warning." —**"Guantánamo Loses 5-Star Rating,"** **6-22-05**

[I]**F** the Democrats and the four pathetic Republicans angling to be called "mavericks" by the **New York Times** really believe we need to treat captured terrorists nicely in order to ensure that the next American they capture will be well treated, then why stop at 600-thread-count sheets for the Guantánamo detainees? We must adopt Sharia law. —**"Are Videotaped Beheadings Covered by Geneva?,"** **9-20-06**

NO cold meals, sleep deprivation, or uncomfortable positions [for Guantánamo

187

detainees]? Obviously, what we need to do is get the U.S. Army to serve drinks on commercial airlines and get the airlines to start supervising the detainees in Guantánamo. —"Losing Their Heads Over Gitmo," 6-15-05

ON the bright side, at least liberals have finally found a group of people in Cuba whom they think deserve to be rescued. —"Guantánamo Loses 5-Star Rating," 6-22-05

GUNS: THE CONSTITUTIONAL RIGHT YOU CAN CARRY IN YOUR PURSE

Mass murderers apparently can't read, since they are constantly shooting up "gun-free zones." With no armed citizen to stop them—because law-abiding citizens are obeying the "Gun-Free Zone" signs—murderers are able to kill unabated, even pausing to reload their weapons, until they get bored and commit suicide or try to escape. Some only stop pulling the trigger when they develop carpal tunnel syndrome.

Contrary to current faddish ideas, we can't identify, much less imprison, "potential" mass murderers. For most such killers, mass murder is their first serious crime. It's not against the law to be crazy—in some jurisdictions it actually makes you more viable as a candidate for public office. The best we can do is enact policies that will reduce the death toll when these acts of carnage occur, as they will in a free and open society of 300 million people, most of whom have cable TV.

Only one policy has ever been shown to deter mass murder: concealed-carry laws. In a comprehensive study of all public, multiple-shooting incidents in America between 1977 and 1999, the estimable economists John Lott Jr. and William Landes found that concealed-carry laws were the only laws that had any beneficial effect on saving lives. And the effect was not insignificant. States that allowed citizens to carry concealed hand-guns reduced multiple-shooting attacks by 60 percent and reduced the death and injury from these attacks by nearly 80 percent.

Among the mass murders at "gun-free zones" in the past decade are these:

- In 2007, a deranged student killed thirty-two people at Virginia Tech—thirty of them in a very short period of time in a single building—before killing himself.

- At the Amish school shooting in 2006, the killer murdered five little girls and then committed suicide.
- At Columbine High School in 1999, two students killed twelve people before ending the carnage themselves by committing suicide.
- In 1998, two students in Craighead County, Arkansas, killed five people, including four little girls, before deciding to attempt an escape.
- In 1996 in Dunblane, Scotland, an adult shooter killed seventeen, then committed suicide. There was no one to stop him.

There was no one to stop any of them.

Contrast these with the school shootings where, by sheer happenstance, a law-abiding citizen at the scene had a gun. The classic case is the shooting at a high school in Santee, California, in 2001. When a student began shooting his classmates, the school promptly activated its "safe-school plan," as the principal later told CNN. Unfortunately, the "safe-school plan" did not involve anyone at the school having a gun. Instead, the school sent in an unarmed "trained campus supervisor" to stop the killer. **Stop it right now or I'll call a "trained campus supervisor"**! The killer promptly shot the "trained campus supervisor." Fortunately, an armed San Diego policeman happened to be bringing his daughter to school that day. He stopped the killer—with a gun—and held him at bay until more police could arrive.

Two dead.

In 2002, an immigrant student in Virginia started shooting his classmates at the Appalachian School of Law. Two of his classmates in another part of the building retrieved guns from their cars, approached the killer, and forced him to drop his weapon, allowing a third classmate to tackle him.

Three dead.

In 1997, a student at Pearl High School in Mississippi had already shot several people at his high school and was headed for the junior high school when assistant principal Joel Myrick retrieved a .45 pistol from his car and pointed it at the gunman's head, ending the slaughter.

Two dead.

A few days later, a student attending a junior high school dance at a restaurant in Edinboro, Pennsylvania, started shooting, whereupon the restaurant owner pulled out his shotgun, chased the gunman from the restaurant, and captured him for the police.
One dead.
When you need a gun, nothing else will do.

GUNS are our friends because in a country without guns, I'm what's known as "prey." All females are. —**"Ruger Is a Girl's Best Friend,"** *George* **magazine, 7-99**

APPARENTLY, even crazy people prefer targets that can't shoot back. The reason schools are consistently popular targets for mass murderers is precisely because of all the idiotic "gun-free school zone" laws. From the people who brought you "zero tolerance," I present the gun-free zone! Yippee! Problem solved! **Bam! Bam! Everybody down! Hey, how did that deranged loner get a gun into this gun-free zone?** . . .

Oh, by the way, the other major "gun-free zone" in America is the post office. —"Let's Make America a 'Sad-Free Zone'!," 4-18-07

[I]T'S difficult to explain why more than 99 percent of people with easy accessibility to guns don't engage in rampage killings, if the problem were the availability of guns. —"It's Sunny Today, So We Need Gun Control," 4-24-00

[W]ITHOUT a gun, crime victims may as well take the advice of Peter Shields, former head of Handgun Control Inc., who recommends that women faced with a rapist or robber "give them what they want." —"For Womb the Bell Tolls," 5-16-00

AS the saying goes: God made man and woman; Colonel Colt made them equal. —"Ruger Is a Girl's Best Friend," *George* magazine, 7-99

IF the courts ever interpreted the Second Amendment the way they interpret the First Amendment, we'd have a right to bear nuclear arms by now. —"Ruger Is a Girl's Best Friend," *George* magazine, 7-99

THE fact that guns can kill another human being is the whole point. That's why they're so darn good at deterring violent criminals. —"For Womb the Bell Tolls," 5-16-00

HOLLYWOOD: THEY OUGHT TO BE COMMITTED— OOPS, THEY ALREADY ARE!

Hollywood actors specialize in dramatizing their heroism in fighting fictional enemies. It is an article of faith in Hollywood, for example, that the all-powerful Ku Klux Klan is still running the state of Mississippi, requiring the film industry to respond with near-fatal doses of self-righteousness. Has anyone in Malibu ever been to Mississippi?

In general, Hollywood actors don't know any facts—but they are 100 percent committed! They feel perfectly comfortable going on TV without knowing any actual information. In their circles, they'll never be challenged on the facts—it's all attitude. You could be literally insane, but if you are a star, people will say, **She's a genius!** Crazy

196

liberal obsessions like global warming take on a life of their own once some idiot celebrity takes up the cause. (Meanwhile, half of Hollywood movies are now made in Canada to avoid the unions.)

Celebrities have influence because going to a Democratic fundraiser in Hollywood is a great way for rich nobodies to mingle with Hollywood glitterati. Liberals' fundraising events are required to have dazzling guest lists like an Oscar party.

> **B-LIST CELEBRITY:** I'm here for the antiwar fundraiser!
> **GUEST LIST CHECKER:** I would know you from . . . ?
> **B-LIST CELEBRITY:** I had a part in **Miami Vice** in 1985.
> **GUEST LIST CHECKER:** I'm sorry, but we're really crowded in here tonight.
> **B-LIST CELEBRITY:** I'm very passionate.
> **GUEST LIST CHECKER:** No, that won't cut it—you'll have to go next door to the annex antiwar meeting.

Unattractive but rich lawyer types pretend to care fervently about the political causes of pulchritudinous retards so they get to hang out with Sharon Stone. They're like the nerdy kid who gets to hang around cool kids because he has a car. Maybe they'll give him a "producer" title if he donates enough money.

ACTORS seem to think they have a constitutional right to say stupid things and have no one criticize them. Public reproach is the equivalent of being thrown in a Gulag. —*Treason,* p. 254

[T]**HE** Democrats are as likely to get tough with Hollywood as Monica was to get tough with Bill Clinton—and for pretty much the same reason. —**"Democrats Worship the Money Shot,"** 9-22-00

Q: How do you empty a room full of rich liberals?
A: Ask for a paternity test.
—**"Checks and Balances, but Mostly Checks,"** 7-31-02

[A]T long last, the "glass ceiling" had been broken [with Halle Berry winning an Oscar]. Large-breasted, slightly cocoa women with idealized Caucasian features finally have a chance in Hollywood! —**"I Like Black People Too, Julia!,"** 4-1-02

[W]ATCHING West Wing . . . you can tell who the Republican is because he always has the bad complexion. —*Kudlow & Company,* 7-3-06

IT'S hard to say whether election night [2004] was worse for Saddam Hussein or Barbra Streisand. Apparently America **doesn't** want to surrender in the War on Terror or outlaw the Pledge of Allegiance. —**"Saddam Charges Voter Intimidation,"** 11-7-02

THE attack of 9/11 was understandably disturbing to celebrities. It created an unpleasant sensation that there was something in the world more important than them and their sybaritic doings in New York nightclubs. —*Treason,* p. 245

HANNITY: [Alec] Baldwin shared a violent fantasy of murdering Osama bin Laden with a box cutter and then it concludes with the following quote: "I gather up the body of the world's most notorious terrorist and hurl it over the balcony. Then, in a final stroke of luck, bin Laden lands on Dick Cheney. . . ."

COULTER: I assume they'd say this is a joke. Except for the part about Alec Baldwin fantasizing about rolling around with swarthy Middle Eastern men. I think he actually does fantasize about that.
—*Hannity & Colmes,* 7-6-06

BEING antiwar in Hollywood was an act of bravery on the order of the keynote speaker at a PLO awards dinner making jokes about Ariel Sharon. —*Treason,* p. 255

IMMIGRATION: THIS IS OURS, THAT IS YOURS . . . SAY, DO YOU DO WINDOWS?

Ninety-five percent of outstanding homicide warrants in Los Angeles are for illegal aliens. But in fairness to the other side's argument, they're coming here to kill people Americans won't kill. That's when you know you have an illegal alien problem: When American murderers are losing their jobs to foreign murderers.

Liberals support the rights of illegal aliens. Also, they threatened to move to France when Bush was reelected. So my proposal is that all liberals leave the United States right now. We'd have more room for illegal aliens here and it would solve Europe's labor shortage. Instead of importing Muslims, Europeans can have our liberals, who share the Muslims' politics but are somewhat less disposed to violence.

O'REILLY: Where do you stand on [illegal aliens] as far as what would you like to see done?

COULTER: I'd build a wall. In fact, I'd hire illegal immigrants to build the wall.
—*The O'Reilly Factor,* 4-13-06

TRY showing up in any other country on the planet, illiterate and penniless, and announcing, "I've seen pictures of your country and it looks great. I think I'd like to live here! Oh, and by the way, would you mind changing all your government and business phone messages, street signs, and ballots into my native language? Thanks!" They would laugh you out of the country.
—"Brown Is the New Black," 4-12-06

IF we're so cruel to minorities, why do they keep coming here? Why aren't they sneaking across the Mexican border to make their way to the Taliban? —"The Mind of a Liberal," 11-15-01

WE fought a civil war to force Democrats to give up on slavery 150 years ago. They've become so desperate for servants that now they're importing an underclass to wash their clothes and pick their vegetables. —"Importing a Slave Class," 5-23-07

[On Senator Harry Reid's claim that an "English-only" amendment is racist]

THAT was a very racist statement, by the way. He gave it in English. I'm offended. I mean, that is excluding people who speak Spanish. That was very racist. —*Hannity & Colmes*, 5-19-06

IF liberals think Iraqis are genetically incapable of pulling off even the most rudimentary form of democracy, why do they believe 50 million Mexicans will magically become good Americans, imbued in the nation's history and culture, upon crossing the Rio Grande? Maybe we should dunk Iraqis in the Rio and see what happens. —"Bush's America: Roach Motel," 6-6-07

PRESIDENT Bush was so buoyed by the warm reception he was given in Albania that he immediately gave all 3 million Albanians American citizenship, provided they learn Spanish. The offer was withdrawn when Bush found out most Albanians haven't broken any U.S. laws. —"No Drug Smuggler Left *Behind!*," 6-13-07

THE AP insanely claimed that the "legal question basically boils down to this: Do immigrants living in the United States legally but without citizenship have the same rights in federal courts as U.S. citizens?" Um, actually, we don't need the Supreme Court to answer that. You just need to think about it for two seconds to realize—the answer is no. Immigrants can be deported. Citizens—even extremely undesirable citizens like reporters—can't be. —"All the News We Get from the ACLU," 4-26-01

WHY not use immigration the way sports teams use the draft—to upgrade our roster? We could take our pick of the world's engineers, doctors, scientists, uh . . . smoking-hot Latin guys who stand around not wearing shirts between workouts. Or, you know, whatever . . . —**"Read My Lips: No New Amnesty,"** 5-17-06

COLMES: Here's my concern: Are they going to be able to have warning signs [at the border] in Spanish, like "Deep Water," or, you know, "No Lifeguard on Duty," or "Curve Ahead"? There's a real safety reason to be able to have . . .

COULTER: How about "No Trespassing" at the border?

COLMES: In Spanish, "Go back to your home country"? That would be okay? All right.

COULTER: We'll also put it in Arabic.
—*Hannity & Colmes,* 5-19-06

IRAQ: A NEW REALITY SHOW

You can never get liberals to focus on the paramount danger of our time, the War on Terror. They will simply respond with meaningless talking points. **The war was phony; where are the WMDs? "Big Oil." Bush is a liar. Halliburton!** In the end, whether we win or lose (the latter is a possibility only if a Democrat becomes president), Democrats will say that's what was going to happen anyway.

Inasmuch as Democrats can't tell voters what they really believe, they all become masters of the Democrat word salad, howling their obscure vexations about bizarre technical issues, managing to sound like they have some thoughtful critique, without ever having a point.

Democrats narrowly won control of Congress in the 2006 midterm elections and immediately became even more hysterical than they are in their natural state. They didn't actually do anything to stop the Iraq War, unless you count their periodic pronouncements that we've lost. (Someone better tell Saddam!)

All the Democratic presidential candidates say the war in Iraq is distracting from the War on Terror. This is like saying the the bombing in Dresden distracted FDR from the war on Nazism.

They all say, "There is no military solution to Iraq; we need a political solution." I don't get that. There can be no "political solution" in Iraq until the Iraqis are safe, which I think requires a military solution. Political solutions tend to present themselves in the wake of military solutions.

How about:

• There is no penal solution to rape, we need a political solution.

- There is no cleaning solution to dirty dishes, we need a political solution.
- There is no educational solution to ignorance, we need a political solution.

Similarly, the Democrats all say, "This is not America's war to win or lose," as Hillary Clinton did on April 26, 2007. (That's Democrat for "I do support the troops!") We've paid half a trillion dollars and three thousand American lives for it so far. If we don't own it, who does? **Will the person who owns this war please use the white courtesy phone?** Say, is Hillary still the smartest woman in the world? Because if she is, I'd like to demand a recount.

It's uncanny, but I believe Hillary's comments about Iraq were George Washington's exact words to his men at Valley Forge: "This is not our war to win or lose, boys." No, my mistake, it wasn't Washington, it was Neville Chamberlain in 1938. Then it turned out there was no political solution, only a military one.

In early 2007, when the new Democratic Congress sent a—promptly vetoed—bill to

President Bush calling for our troops to be withdrawn from Iraq, B. Hussein Obama said, "We are one signature away from ending this war." Unless the "one signature" he was hoping for was that of Osama bin Laden's on a surrender document, "one signature" would not end the war. It would merely return us to the days when only one side was fighting.

Who do they think is being fooled by this claptrap—I mean, besides Dennis Kucinich? I note that the same celebrities and academics hysterically demanding that we pull out of Iraq because we're putting our troops in the middle of a civil war are demanding we send troops uninvited into Darfur into the middle of a civil war. I haven't heard a single Darfur "exit strategy" from the whole lot of them.

Was the war in Iraq worth it? Hmmm . . . I'm not sure. I know! Let's ask the 50 million people, half of them women and girls, who no longer live under brutal Islamic tyranny thanks to the U.S. military. Maybe they would know!

IN response to Bush's ultimatum, Saddam's son Uday Hussein said Bush was stupid. He said Bush wanted to attack Iraq because of his family. And he said American boys would die. At least someone is finding the **New York Times** editorial page helpful these days. —"Kissing Cousins: New York Literati and Nazis," 3-20-03

Q: Could you give us two or three examples of people on the left who acted unpatriotically during the Iraq War (or the buildup to it) and tell us what they did that was unpatriotic?

A: Better yet, for a complete list just go to the DNC website, the Screen Actors Guild membership site, and the op-ed page of the **New York Times** (minus Bill Safire).
—Interview, *Right Wing News*, 6-03

THESE Democrats want to have it both ways. If the war goes well—a lot of them voted for war with Iraq, didn't they? But if the war does not go well, many of the very Democrats who voted for the war resolution will have emerged as leading spokesmen for the antiwar position. A vote for the war, surrounded by Neville Chamberlain foot-dragging, is a fraud. —"War-Torn Democrats," 1-30-03

[LIBERALS] made the singular argument that only the rich clamored for war with Iraq because their children wouldn't fight it. If only the rich were for the war, Central Park West and Amagansett would have been ablaze with war fever as peace marches swept through humble middle-class neighborhoods. —*Treason*, p. 216

MORALITY matters, not polls. In 1938, the polls were not very strong for doing anything in World War II. I think polls are really irrelevant as a moral matter. —*Hannity & Colmes*, 1-23-03

IN the Democrats' worst-case scenario, the United States would be acting precipitately to remove a ruthless dictator who tortured his own people. It's not as if anyone was worried we were making a horrible miscalculation and were about to depose the Iraqi Abraham Lincoln. (Although Baath Party legend has it that a young Saddam once trudged twenty miles round-trip through the snow to rape and dismember a woman.) —*Treason*, p. 228

WHEN the story first broke [that Saddam had been captured] I had the TV on with the sound off. I saw the footage of that filthy, hairy, unshaven creature looking dazed and out of it and I thought: "My God, they've arrested Nick Nolte again!" —Interview, FrontPage Magazine, 12-23-03

SAY, has anyone asked Dick Gephardt if this falls under "miserable failure"? —"It's Like Christmas in December!," 12-18-03

I HAD mixed feelings about Saddam's capture—sort of a combination of unbridled joy and hysterical elation. Pity it wasn't a week or so earlier, though. Hussein might have made the cut as one of Barbara Walters's "ten most fascinating people of 2003." —Interview, FrontPage Magazine, 12-23-03

[Y]OU'D have to put liberals in Abu Ghraib to get them to tell the truth about what people were saying before the war—and then the problem would be that most liberals would enjoy those activities. —**"This Is History Calling—Quick, Get Me a Rewrite!,"** 6-3-04

ALL the Democrats oppose the war. And all the Democrats who took a position on the war before it began were for it, but now believe that everything Bush did from that moment forward has been bad! bad! bad! This is with the exception of Joe Lieberman, who, as an observant Jew, is forbidden to backpedal after sundown on Fridays. —**"In Search of the Better 'Phony American,'"** 1-22-04

MILLIONS of Iraqis voted in a free and democratic election in January—men, women, and an estimated 2,000 confused elderly voters in Palm Beach. —**Speech, University of Texas-Austin, 5-4-05**

Q: Is it possible to export democracy?
A: Yes. Ever heard of "Italy"?
　　—**Interview,** *Il Foglio* **(Italy), 10-04**

TEDDY KENNEDY: APPARENTLY FAT, DRUNK, AND STUPID IS A WAY TO GO THROUGH LIFE

They named airports, theaters, space centers, and roads after John F. Kennedy, whereas the only thing named after Ted Kennedy is a bridge.

In 1969, married U.S. senator Ted Kennedy killed Mary Jo Kopechne when he drove his car off the Chappaquiddick bridge following a party on Martha's Vineyard. Kennedy escaped the car and left Mary Jo behind, where she was trapped in the car and drowned. He then returned to his hotel to engage in ostentatious behavior to create an alibi for the time of the accident. Since no one else would take responsibility for his accident, Kennedy was eventually forced to admit he was the driver of the car that plunged Mary Jo Kopechne to her death. Luckily for him, the Kennedys have diplomatic immunity in Massachusetts, so he only pled guilty to a minor infraction and never served a day in jail.

In 1980—just a little more than ten years after he killed Kopechne—Teddy Kennedy ran for president. After running in the 1960 presidential election, Richard Nixon went on an eight-year hiatus just for losing an election. The Chappaquiddick incident seems to have colored the morals of the entire Democratic Party. The party has become practiced at defending the indefensible. One imagines Bill Clinton thinking to himself in 1998, **Screw it—if Teddy could ride out Chappaquiddick, I'll be damned if I'm going to resign over Monica.**

IF the Democrats want to stay in the middle of the road, why do they keep sticking with Teddy Kennedy? Didn't he have some trouble staying in the middle of the road? **—Speech, Boston College, 11-19-04**

TEDDY Kennedy crawls out of Boston Harbor with a quart of Scotch in one pocket and a pair of pantyhose in the other, and Democrats hail him as their party's spiritual leader. —*How to Talk to a Liberal (If You Must)*, p. 322

[CHERNOBYL] was the worst nuclear disaster in history—**finally** giving us a nuclear power plant that killed more people than died in Teddy Kennedy's car. —*Godless*, p. 6

IT'S not as if Democrats can say: **Okay, okay! The man paid a price! Let it go!** He didn't pay a price. The Kopechne family paid a price. Kennedy weaved away scot-free. —" 'Chocolate City' Sprinkled with Nuts," 1-19-06

MAYBE there's a better committee for Senator Drunkennedy to sit on—one that does not require constant moral grandstanding from the Democrats. Fortunately for the Democrats, People For the American Way holds the copyright to the words "troubling" and "concerned." I bet Mary Jo Kopechne was "troubled" and "concerned" about the senator leaving her trapped in a car underwater while he went back to the hotel to create an alibi. —*Godless*, p. 90

TED Kennedy gave a speech last week in which he called the liberation of Iraq a "political product." Then again, Ted Kennedy calls Chivas Regal "that life-sustaining liquid." —**"What Happened to Your Queer Party-Friends?,"** 1-21-04

KENNEDY insists that Kerry "just won't talk about" Vietnam. Apparently Vietnam was a brief, death-defying interlude that Kerry would simply prefer not to discuss. You might say it's his Chappaquiddick. —**"Boobs in the News,"** 2-4-04

CAN'T we rustle up a right-wing prosecutor to indict Teddy Kennedy for Mary Jo Kopechne's drowning? Unlike the cases against [Rush] Limbaugh and [Tom] DeLay, Mary Jo's death was arguably a crime, and we could probably prove it in court. —**"Why Can't I Get Arrested?,"** 12-14-05

[On Congressman Patrick Kennedy's 3 a.m. car crash on Capitol Hill]

LET'S just hope Teddy Kennedy can loan him that fake neck brace. —*Hannity & Colmes,* 5-5-06

JOHN KERRY: "WHO AMONG US DOES NOT LOVE NASCAR?"*

John Kerry is a metaphor for liberals writing history. Here is my script for a short film of John Kerry in Vietnam:

> **SWIFTIE #1:** Do I have to write the after-action report? I wanted to take a nap.
>
> **KERRY:** I'll write it!
>
> **SWIFTIE #1:** Really? But you always write the after-action reports.
>
> **KERRY:** No really, I don't mind!
>
> **SWIFTIE #2:** Take a night off. Come have a beer with us.
>
> **KERRY:** No, no, I don't mind, I'll stay late. *(Later that night, at typewriter,*

---

*Quoted in the **New York Times,** August 22, 2004.

writing): "While others ran, I coura-
geously stood my ground. . . ."

End of short film.

Based on his vast military experience typ-
ing up after-action reports (in which he always performed heroically), Kerry spent the
2004 presidential campaign attacking the
troops. On CBS's **Face the Nation with
Bob Schieffer,** Kerry said, "There is no reason, Bob, that young American soldiers
need to be going into the homes of Iraqis in
the dead of night, terrorizing kids and children, you know, women, breaking sort of
the customs of the—historical customs, religious customs, whether you like it or not.
Iraqis should be doing that."

John Kerry, reporting for duty.

I know everyone else was mesmerized
by Kerry's claim that American troops were
"terrorizing" Iraqis, which was every bit as
credible as his claim that American GIs were
committing war crimes during the Vietnam
War, in the sense that he didn't see those
atrocities, either. But I was interested in a
different part of Kerry's statement.

He said that American GIs are—I quote— "terrorizing kids and children." So they're terrorizing children—**and kids, too?** Wait until PETA hears about this. Because terrorizing baby goats is clearly a violation of the Geneva Conventions. Can you imagine the hoots of derision if Bush had said "kids and children"? Michael Moore would get a whole movie out of it.

COLMES: Ann, you referred to John Kerry as a kept man, a gigolo, and a cad. Those are just three things.

COULTER: No one has contested me on the facts, I notice.

—*Hannity & Colmes*, 1-28-04

Q: If Kerry should win, what will the changes in the U.S.A. be?

A: He's got this exciting new plan for Iraq I think you Italians may have heard of. It's called "unconditional surrender."

—Interview, *Il Foglio* (Italy), 10-04

Q: What would it be like dating Kerry?

A: Quite a bore. You'd have to get approval from the UN Security Council before making a move. You'd be stuck in one of those dinky little hybrid cars, but maybe his **"family"** would have a nice method of transportation.
—Interview, *New York Observer*, 9-13-04

[**AN** article in the **Washington Post** said:] "This was Primal John . . . who ran with the bulls at Pamplona and, when trampled, got up, chased the bull, and grabbed for its horns." (I'm almost sure this was a polite reference to John and Teresa's honeymoon night.) —**"Ballad of the French Berets,"** 8-18-04

AT the 2003 reunion of Swift Boat Veterans about 300 men showed up: 85 percent of them think Kerry is unfit to be president. (But on the bright side, Kerry was voted, in absentia, "Most Likely to Run for President on His Phony War Record.") —**"Brothers Band Together Against Kerry,"** 8-10-04

THE media will spend weeks going through pay stubs for Bush's National Guard service in Alabama in the waning days of war, but if Kerry tells them exotic tales of covert missions into Cambodia directed by Richard Nixon, they don't even bother to fact-check who was president in December 1968. —**"Ballad of the French Berets,"** **8-18-04**

KERRY's speechwriters are now throwing key words like "future" and "freedom" together in various combinations in hopes of stumbling upon something the senator actually believes in just by random chance. —**"Fall Fashion Preview: Cowboy Boots In, Flip-Flops Out,"** **10-13-04**

SO now there actually are two leaders backing up John Kerry's claim that foreign leaders support him: a Socialist terrorist-appeaser [Spanish Prime Minister José Zapatero] and [Kim Jong Il] a Marxist mass murderer who dresses like Bea Arthur. —**"Al Qaeda Barks, the Spanish Fly,"** **3-17-04**

IF John Kerry had a dollar for every time he bragged about serving in Vietnam—Oh wait, he does. —"American Women to Kerry: We Don't Think You're So Hot Either," 5-8-03

KERRY is demanding to be made president on the basis of spending four months in Vietnam thirty-five years ago. And yet the men who know what he did during those four months don't think he's fit to be dogcatcher. That seems newsworthy to me, but I must be wrong, since the media have engineered a total blackout of the Swift Boat Veterans. —"Brothers Band Together Against Kerry," 8-10-04

POSSIBLE slogan: "Kerry—The Same as Clinton, Without the Burning Sensation." —"40 Excuses and a Mule," 10-27-04

LIKE every war hero I've ever met, John Kerry seems content to spend his days bragging about his battlefield exploits. Wait, wait . . . let me correct that last sentence: Like **no** war hero I've ever met. —*How to Talk to a Liberal (If You Must)*, p. 108

[JOHN] Kerry was in Vietnam for only four months, which, coincidentally, is less than the combined airtime he's spent talking about it. —"Brothers Band Together Against Kerry," 8-11-04

IN liberals' defense, they've got a better shot at convincing Americans that Bush is responsible for a hurricane than convincing them that John Kerry was fit to be commander in chief. Compared to Kerry, Katrina is a blowhard they can work with. —"Actually, 'Judicial Activism' Means 'E = mc²,'" 9-14-05

HANNITY: If "W" [in "George W. Bush"] stands for wrong, what should "F" [in "John F. Kerry"] stand for, flip-flop? You like that, Richard Aborn?

Democratic strategist RICHARD ABORN: Well, it doesn't stand for furious. We're a little more restrained than that, contrary to what you might wish.

COULTER: That wasn't the word we were thinking of.

—Hannity & Colmes, 9-7-04

THE LANGUAGE POLICE:
CAN'T WE HAVE MORE REAL POLICE?

Liberals are obsessed with language and controlling the words people use. If they can control our words, they can control us. They simultaneously promote as many languages as possible in America—other than English—and frantically censor words and speakers. Soon the only two words we'll be allowed to use are: "I'm offended." **("Estoy offendido.")**

While most people think it would be a good idea for immigrants to a new country to learn the native language, this would be a disaster for the Democrats. They don't do well when the electorate understands what they're talking about. Ideally, the Democrats should run campaign advertising in another language, perhaps German. But short of that, their best hope is to have lots and lots of voters who don't speak English. They insist on having ballots in Urdu, but I'm pretty sure we won't be hearing any Urdu spoken on the Senate floor.

For English speakers, the Democratic Party has created a secret vocabulary. "Civil rights," "science," "constitutional rights," "moderate," "extremist," "peace"—in standard Democrat usage, none of these words mean what normal people would think they mean. Of course, they also claim not to know what "liberal" means. It is the opposite of "conservative," which means "someone who doesn't spit in a person's face for requesting a religious donation."

When referring to the 9/11 terrorists, Reuters news service will only use the words "terror" and "terrorists" in quotation marks, because, its global news editor said, "one man's terrorist is another man's freedom fighter." The AP photo bank titles a photo of Osama bin Laden "Exiled Saudi dissident Osama bin Laden." I guess we've come a long way since the people shooting at us could be called "nips," "krauts," or "the yellow peril." Now we must be linguistically sensitive toward our enemies.

This isn't nonjudgmentalism; it's taking sides against the West. Soon Reuters was running photo captions with statements like this: "Human rights around the world have been a casualty of the U.S. 'war on terror' since September 11." Changing words quickly metastasizes into changing facts. The late liberal lawyer William Kunstler said, "It makes no difference anymore whether the attack on Tawana [Brawley] really happened. It doesn't disguise the fact that a lot of young black women are treated the way she said she was treated." Name one.

There will be huge heaping hunks of judgmentalism shown toward the economically advantaged, patriarchal white-male oppressor class. You know, people like me.

In 2005, the British Professional Association of Teachers proposed banning the word "failed" from English classrooms in order to avoid labeling children, insisting that the word "failed" should be replaced with "deferred success." Following the English lead, perhaps French history textbooks could now be rewritten to herald France's many military "deferred victories."

As for my own—as yet—uncensored language, you'd have to be either retarded or work for the Soviet thought police not to understand that much of what I say is a joke (admittedly, never as funny as the reaction). But apparently, in the early sixties and seventies, a medical procedure used to be performed whereby a person's humor was removed at birth. Fortunately, this practice was outlawed years ago, but you still see a few such people wandering around, helpless in the world of rhetoric. They simply lack the enzyme that detects irony. These are the kind of people who say, "What do you mean 'is it hot enough for me?' I hate it this hot!"

The language police are overpaid, and there are too many of them. Can't we have more regular police?

THAT'S the difference between conservatives and liberals. I'm ticked off when people don't quote me accurately. They're ticked off when people **do** quote them accurately. —Interview, *New York Observer,* 7-3-06

THESE are the rules—and pay close attention, because they are completely arbitrary: "Dixie" is bad because it uses Southern black dialect. Rap music, however, is good, even though it employs a criminal black dialect. The flag under which slavery flourished for almost a century is good. But the flag under which slavery existed for less than a decade is bad. One continent's slavery is good, but another continent's purchasing of those very slaves is bad. And for the final rousing conclusion: The party that supported slavery, leading to the Civil War, is good. But the party that was created expressly to oppose slavery is bad. —"A Confederacy of Dunces," 2-1-00

LIBERALS' idea of civil discourse is no conservatives talking. —*The Matt Drudge Show,* 6-11-06

LIBERALS . . . refuse to acknowledge the meaning of "labels," which are nothing more than truths liberals don't like. They especially hate the word "liberal." Everyone knows it's an insult to be called a liberal, widely understood to connote a dastardly individual. —*Slander*, p. 123

THE use of language is "name-calling." Harpies and witches is what I think [the Jersey Girls] are, which is why I used those words. And I must say, I certainly have spotlighted the issue with my alleged "name-calling." The entire country is now riveted on the Left's device of using victims to advance their half-baked, unsalable ideas. From now on, every time the Left showcases another sobbing, hysterical woman as its spokesperson, people will say, "Gosh, she looks like she's having a good time." So I'd say my "name-calling" has been a smashing success. And by the way, I've got a few more names in my bag. —Interview, *Time*, 6-8-06

IT'S difficult to have a simple conversation, much less engage in free-ranging, open scientific inquiry, when liberals are constantly rushing in with their rule book about what can and cannot be said. —*Godless*, p. 175

IT was not until the war on terrorism that liberals' use of "primitive" as an epithet for right-wingers finally fell out of fashion, presumably in deference to the feelings of an enemy that travels by camel. —*Treason*, p. 149

COLMES: You understand that phrase "swarthy males" can be offensive to some people?
COULTER: No. Actually, I rather like swarthy males.
    —*Hannity & Colmes*, 10-2-01

"**CONTROVERSIAL**" means "telling the truth about liberals." It is one of the words, along with "shrill" and "divisive," that liberals apply to conservatives before blacklisting them. —*Treason*, p. 30

WHAT liberals mean by "goose-stepping" and "ethnic cleansing" is generally along the line of "eliminating taxpayer funding for the National Endowment for the Arts." But they can't say that, or people would realize they're crazy. —*Slander*, p. 12

"**STUPID**" means one thing: "threatening to the interests of the Democratic Party." The more conservative the Republican, the more vicious and hysterical the attacks on his intelligence will be. Liberals have not only run out of arguments, they've run out of adjectives. —*Slander,* p. 125

LIBERALS can lie under oath in legal proceedings and it's a "personal matter." Conservatives must scream their every failing from the rooftops or they are "liars." —*How to Talk to a Liberal (If You Must),* p. 155

LIKE the words "diverse" and "tolerance," "free speech" means nothing but "Shut up, we win." It's free speech (for liberals), diversity (of liberals), and tolerance (toward liberals). —**"Not Crazy Horse, Just Crazy,"** 2-17-05

LIBERALS use the word "science" exactly as they use the word "constitutional." Both words are nothing more or less than a general statement of liberal approval, having nothing to do with either science or the

Constitution. (Thus, for example, the following sentence makes sense to liberals: **President Clinton saved the Constitution by repeatedly ejaculating on a fat Jewish girl in the Oval Office.**) —*Godless*, pp. 3-4

EVERY single Democrat called Saddam Hussein "despicable." "Despicable" is evidently what Democrats call problems they have no intention of addressing. Republicans should start referring to inadequate arts funding and large class size as "despicable." —*Treason*, p. 204

KIND and well-meaning people find themselves afraid to talk about politics. Any sentient person has to be concerned that he might innocently make an argument or employ a turn of phrase that will be discerned by the liberal cult as a "code word" evincing a genocidal tendency. The only safe course is to be consciously, stultifyingly boring. —*Slander*, p. 3

THE New York Times and the rest of the mainstream media will only refer to partial birth abortion as "what its opponents refer to as partial birth abortion." What do its supporters call it? Casual Fridays? Bean-with-bacon potato chip dip? Uh . . . Steve? —*Godless*, p. 79

THERE is more variation among dogs than among liberals, but that doesn't mean the word "dog" has no meaning. No one demands a twenty-minute exegesis on the differences between a poodle and a Great Dane before acknowledging that the word "dog" has meaning. Similarly, there are tall liberals, short liberals, cowardly liberals, even more cowardly liberals—but there is still an essential dogness to all of them. —*Slander*, p. 123

IF Democrats ever dared speak coherently about what they believe, the American people would lynch them. —*Godless*, p. 19

LIBERAL "ARGUMENT": HISSING, SCRATCHING, AND HAIR-PULLING

For reasons I cannot understand, liberals are **still** speaking out on public issues. If you must talk to liberals, I advise using a whip and a chair. Under no circumstances should you use big concepts—don't even use big words. And speak as fast as possible, so you can make your main points before they start screaming. They are cackling hens with absolutely no leadership abilities, but periodically they try to peck someone to death.

LIBERALS can never just make a principled argument. It has to be Bambi against

Hitler. —"The Trillion-Dollar Loophole in 'Campaign Finance Reform,'" 3-22-01

[W]HEN every one of your arguments is characterized as an attempt to bring about slavery or resegregate lunch counters, it's a little hard to have any sort of productive debate. —*Today* show, 6-26-02

POLITICAL "debate" in this country is insufferable. Whether conducted in Congress or on the political talk shows, or played out at dinners and cocktail parties, politics is a nasty sport. At the risk of giving away the ending: It's all liberals' fault. —*Slander,* p. 1

LIBERALS are always playacting that they are under some monstrous attack from the right wing as they insouciantly place all Americans in danger. Their default position is umbrage, bordering on high dudgeon. —"*N.Y. Times:* Better Dead Than Read," 7-13-06

LIBERALS have managed to eliminate the idea of manly honor. Instead, all they

have is womanly indignation. —*Hannity &
Colmes*, 6-7-06

[**JOSEPH**] Welch's performance at the
Army-McCarthy hearings is the essence of
liberal argumentation. Welch would say
something vicious, McCarthy would reply,
and Welch would start crying. This is why
no woman worth her salt ever loses an
argument. —*Treason*, p. 116

IF liberals cared about ideas or knew any
facts, they would cease being liberals.
—"Give Us 22 Minutes, We'll Give Up the
Country," 2-20-03

LIBERALS' idea of a good retort to a conservative argument is to investigate your
personal life and find out if you're into
S&M. —*How to Talk to a Liberal (If You
Must)*, p. 14

THE only proven method for a Republican to avoid having his name turned into
a liberal malediction is to be completely
ineffective. You'll notice there's no "Stop

Lamar Alexander Before It's Too Late" website. —"Liberal War on Terrorism Heats Up: Tom DeLay Finally Captured," 4-5-06

WHEN did that enter the public debate—that someone is "mean"? We're having an argument, I'm winning, and they sit back and cry and say, "Oh, you're **mean.**" When did that happen? —Interview, *New York Observer,* 7-3-06

I ALWAYS feel like I'm explaining "Why is a raisin not like an elephant?" to Democrats. Yes, these are different. —*Hannity & Colmes,* 8-31-06

CONSERVATIVES are required to lose an argument on purpose whenever some liberal starts sniffling. It's their obligation to let liberals have the last word. —*Treason,* p. 119

OFTEN short on details, the classic liberal response to a principled conservative argument is to accuse Republicans of planning a second Holocaust. —*Slander,* p. 8

A LITTLE variation in epithets would at least create the illusion of having an argument. "Nazi" can be used properly in a sentence, but it tends to lose its sting when you call every Republican a Nazi. . . . Using the same words to describe school vouchers as to characterize the Holocaust tends to leave the impression that you forgot your point. —*Slander,* p. 20

EVEN when liberals are trying to show their moderate, country-music-loving side by claiming to oppose having sex with the family dog, they can't formulate a logical argument to explain why not. The idea of objective truth handed down from the God of Abraham makes them squirm. So they just assert what they assert is true because they assert it. It's no wonder liberals' default argument is to throw food. —*Godless,* p. 279

I WATCHED all these other authors being interviewed and asked about their books. Nobody says to the author of **Thomas Jefferson: A Life,** "Did you just do this to

make money? Why'd you use this word rather than that word? Isn't that **mean?**"
—Interview, *New York Observer,* 7-3-06

ANOTHER infantile trope of the left is to deny the relevance of analogies and categories, so you can never trap them. No matter how apt it is, no matter how clearly it exposed the poverty of their logic, liberals always say analogies have "changed the subject": **We were talking about Paula Jones, so I don't know where Anita Hill came from.**
—*Slander,* p. 123

IF liberals were prevented from ever again calling Republicans dumb, they would be robbed of half their arguments. To be sure, they would still have "racist," "fascist," "homophobe," "ugly," and a few other highly nuanced arguments in the quiver.
—*Slander,* p. 121

WHENEVER liberals are frustrated, they accuse their opponents of "xenophobia"—which is admittedly a step up from Muslims who express frustration by strapping dynamite to children. —"French Voters Tentatively Reject Dynamiting Notre Dame," 5-5-02

LIBERALS simply refuse to consider thoughts that would interfere with their lemming-like groupthink. They hold their hands over their ears like little children who don't want to listen to Mother. —"Liberal Arguments: Still a Quagmire," 8-28-03

DEPLOYING their usual fallacy of composition, liberals say that because they have a constitutional right to say stupid things, the stupid things they say must have merit. . . . Yes, Democrats are constitutionally entitled to be stupid. They are, after all, Democrats. But they're wrong and everyone knows it—including them. —*Godless,* p. 141

WHENEVER a liberal begins a statement with "I don't know which is more frightening," you know the answer is going to be pretty clear. —*Treason,* p. 6

LIBERALS never argue with one another over substance; their only dispute is how to prevent the public from figuring out what they really believe. —*How to Talk to a Liberal (If You Must)*, p. 322

CONSERVATIVES live under a jurisprudence of laws, but they get prosecuted under liberals' jurisprudence of epithets. — "Liberal War on Terrorism Heats Up: Tom DeLay Finally Captured," 4-5-06

IT is important to remember that when arguing with liberals, you are always within inches of the "Arab street." Liberals traffic in shouting and demagogy. In a public setting, they will work themselves into a dervish-like trance and start incanting inanities: "BUSH LIED, KIDS DIED!" "RACIST!" "FASCIST!" "FIRE RUMSFELD!" "HALLIBURTON!" Fortunately, the street performers usually punch themselves out eventually and are taken back to their parents' house. —*How to Talk to a Liberal (If You Must)*, p. 1

[T]HE Democrats hit on an ingenious strategy: They would choose only messengers whom we're not allowed to reply to. That's why Democratic spokesmen these days are sobbing, hysterical women. You can't respond to them because that would be questioning the authenticity of their suffering. —*Godless*, p. 101

PERHAPS the Democrats could find an orphaned child whose parents were brutally hacksawed to death to put forth their tax plan. —*Godless*, p. 146

IF you can somehow force a liberal into a point-counterpoint argument, his retorts will bear no relation to what you said— unless you were, in fact, talking about your looks, your age, your weight, your personal obsessions, or whether you are a fascist. —*How to Talk to a Liberal (If You Must)*, p. 3

COLMES: How do you talk to a liberal?
COULTER: I practice with you and other five-year-olds.
—*Hannity & Colmes*, 6-14-04

LIBERALISM AND OTHER PSYCHOLOGICAL DISORDERS

Among the most peculiar psychological compulsions of the modern liberal is his tendency toward conspiracy theories. The liberal will stay up at night making weird connections, such as that ABC corporation is owned by DEF company, which is a subdivision of XYZ corporation, which is owned by a golf partner of George Bush's father.

The company that screened voting lists in Florida was . . . based in Texas!

Listen, I don't want you home alone tonight.

They believe all corporations are genetically linked. Giant corporations may own hundreds of subsidiary companies. But to liberals, it's all the same corporation, and

245

the CEO of General Electric is controlling the opening monologue on **Saturday Night Live.**

Any mention of a corporation is ipso facto sinister, because liberals subscribe to the crazy Marxist notion that corporations are conservative, despite the blindingly obvious fact that the vast majority of Fortune 500 CEOs are liberals.

Of hundreds of companies that could provide support services in Iraq, isn't it suspicious that Halliburton got the government contract?

Try asking the follow-up question: Exactly how many companies can provide these services? Answer: Two. The other one is Schlumberger, a French company. After liberal hysteria produced congressional investigations into Halliburton's contracts in Iraq, Congress's Government Accountability Office confirmed that Halliburton was the only American company that could provide the necessary oil field services after the invasion of Iraq. Oh also, Halliburton is losing money in Iraq. That's how powerful the military-industrial complex is.

This is like saying, "Isn't it interesting that—without exception—the World Series has had teams from the American League every year? I believe we're looking at a conspiracy, gentlemen." No, actually it's not that weird. There are only two leagues. But this is the kind of thinking you get on the left these days.

LIBERALISM is a mental defect. Liberals are racked by self-loathing as the result of some traumatic incident—say, driving drunk off a bridge with your mistress passed out in the back seat and letting the poor girl drown because you're a married man and a U.S. senator, just to take one utterly random, hypothetical example off the top of my head. —Interview, FrontPage Magazine, 1-12-04

IN the history of the nation, there has never been a political party so ridiculous as today's Democrats. It's as if all the brain-damaged people in America got together and formed a voting bloc. —"Fork Replaces Donkey as Democratic Party Symbol," 1-11-06

LIBERALS are incapable of embarrassment—they're like Arabs without the fighting spirit. —"My Name Is Adolf," 9-12-02

MATT Drudge is evidently accused of extracting semen from Bill Clinton and placing it on Monica Lewinsky's dress. That is what liberals believe psychologically: They simply feel that Drudge's scoop on Clinton's "essence" should have been false, just like the Tawana Brawley hoax should have been true. —*Slander*, p. 92

LIBERALS love conspiracy theories almost as much as Arabs do. Only a vast conspiracy could explain why they are so unpopular with Americans. (Liberals, I mean. Not Arabs. Everybody knows why Arabs aren't popular with Americans.) —*Godless* (paperback), p. 296

THE imminence of conservative victory has driven liberals to insanity. Have I

contributed to this? Gosh, I hope so.
—Interview, *Baltimore Sun,* 7-30-06

WHERE there is a vacuum of ideas, paranoia slips in. Much of the Left's hate speech bears greater similarity to a psychological disorder than to standard political discourse. —*Slander,* p. 199

LIBERALS are the only known species whose powers of reasoning are not improved by the benefit of hindsight. Not only are they always fighting the last war, in most cases they're surrendering. —"Even with Hindsight They Can't See Straight," 5-6-04

SOME liberals have become even too crazy for Texas to execute, which is a damn shame. —Speech, University of Texas-Austin, 5-4-05

A CENTRAL component of liberal hate speech is to make paranoid accusations based on their own neurotic impulses, such as calling Republicans angry, hate-filled, and mean. . . . There is maybe just the tiniest element of projection and compulsion in all this. —*Slander,* p. 19

LIBERALS are not just afraid of reading my books, they're afraid of other people reading my books. . . . What they'd really like to do is burn all of my books, except that might contribute to global warming. —Interview, *Human Events,* 6-29-06

LIBERALS hate America, they hate "flag-wavers," they hate abortion opponents, they hate all religions except Islam (post 9/11). Even Islamic terrorists don't hate America like liberals do. They don't have the energy. If they had that much energy, they'd have indoor plumbing by now. —*Slander,* p. 6

I'M not a psycho-biographer. I'll leave it to others to explore why even those Democrats who appear to be genuinely patriotic—and we don't see so many of those anymore—still manage to screw up foreign policy every bit as much as Howard Dean would. (I would imagine their deeply felt need for approval from the French would figure into any psychological profile.) —FrontPage Magazine, 12-23-03

OBVIOUSLY, I engage in a lot of invective. But liberals can't tell the difference between invective that's true and invective that isn't true. —Interview, *Telegraph* (U.K.), 7-19-02

THE only people whom liberals absolutely refuse to hold accountable for anything are their friends the Islamofascists. —"Battered Republican Syndrome," 8-28-03

[L]IBERALISM is a whimsical luxury of the very rich—and the very poor, both of whom have little stake in society. —*Slander,* p. 31

THE liberals are having a spirited debate on whether it's appropriate for liberal males to fantasize about raping Ann Coulter. And the feminists aren't quite sure, because generally, they're against rape, but they're considering making an exception in this one case. —*The O'Reilly Factor,* 12-1-05

IF you threw a glass of cold water on a liberal in the middle of a sound sleep, he'd jerk awake denouncing the religious right. —*Slander*, p. 167

READ the **New York Times** letters to the editor—it's all the same thing. It's always, "I'm shocked," "I'm appalled," "I'm bewildered," "I'm frightened," because John Ashcroft is "frightening," "shocking," "bewildering," "perplexing"! You read through the letters to the editor right now in the war on terrorism, and you realize how the myth of McCarthyism was created—this idea that people were terrified, frightened—because this is what letter writers to the **New York Times** are saying every single day! It's my favorite section of the paper, other than the obituaries. —Interview, *New York Observer*, 8-25-03

THERE'S no consensus position, but the Democrats are pretty sure the real reason we went to Iraq was one of the following:

- Bush family's connections to the Saudis

- Halliburton
- The Carlyle Group
- something about the Texas Rangers needing more left-handed pitching
- the neoconservatives
- the Straussians
- oil
- the Jews
- oily Jews

This may be the first time in American history that the decisional calculus for many voters will be: Do I really want to throw my hat in with these crazy people?
—"Inmates 'Have a Plan' to Run the Asylum," 10-21-04

SENSING a potential blowout catastrophe for the Democratic Party, liberals seem to be trying to warn us: "One got loose! If you spot Dr. Dean, take no action yourself. Contact the DNC immediately."
—Speech, CPAC, 2-25-03

I ALWAYS thought it would be thrilling to be a liberal. Because I'm a cranky conservative, the world simply reinforces my prejudices on a daily basis. But for liberals,

everything is always an exciting surprise.
—"Liberals Shocked: Impeached Felon Took Ottoman," 2-11-01

Q: Would you argue that leftism/liberalism is ultimately, in most cases, the depersonalization and politicization of personal neuroses?

A: Pause for a moment to consider the probable mental state of Howard Dean and then ask me that question again.
—Interview, FrontPage Magazine, 12-23-03

"LIBERAL PATRIOTISM" AND OTHER OXYMORONS

If a genie offered me only one wish in this life, it would be to have a TV show where I'd get to interview liberal celebrities while they are strapped to lie-detector machines. I would ask them questions like "Do you believe in a Supreme Being?" and "Do you love your country?" My guests would include Hillary Clinton, Barbara Boxer, Bill Clinton, Maureen Dowd, Mario Cuomo, Nancy Pelosi—the whole phony bunch.

There's nothing deceptive about my show, they couldn't go to jail for lying, and I wouldn't be invading their privacy. Oh, and I'd be hooked up, too! I would only ask liberals questions about things they publicly profess to believe. They say they love America; I simply don't believe them.

EVERYONE says liberals love America too. No, they don't.—*Treason*, **p. 1**

IF they are not traitors, how do we tell the difference? How does an adult tell the difference between someone who is constantly rooting against his own country, who does not want America to go clear out the swamps that produced the terrorists of 9/11, who scream about a civil liberties emergency in America whenever anyone scowls at a Muslim? What is their point? — *Scarborough Country*, 6-25-03

ROBERT NOVAK: Do we have some good [liberals] who do love their country, even though they may have the wrong solutions for it?

COULTER: There is Zell Miller, and then I run out of names.
—*Crossfire*, 6-30-03

LIBERALS are like New York cabdrivers who never see the red light coming. Other people slow down as they see the yellow. New York cabdrivers are going 60 miles an hour—RED! **Aahhhhhhhh!** That's the Democrats with an imminent threat: "No, it's not imminent, it's not imminent—oh, there's a missile headed for Chicago!" **Now** they'll say it's imminent. Well, thanks! **Thanks** for that. **Thank** you. —Interview, *New York Observer*, 7-3-06

THE Left's idea of winning the Cold War was a nuclear freeze, opposing anti-Communist guerrillas all over the world, opposing the liberation of Grenada, opposing a missile defense shield, and engaging in sweet talk with the Kremlin. They never explained how their plan would work— but the French were impressed. —*Treason*, p. 181

I HAVE to go through fifty years of [the Democrats' history] to make my point. It's not on this issue or that issue. It is a consistent pattern of constantly rooting against America's best interests. And you know, for the first twenty, thirty years, you might say they were just mistaken. But after fifty years of it, a pattern starts to develop. —*Scarborough Country, 7-7-03*

Q: What is the most important lesson Americans can learn from our experience in Vietnam?

A: If you can possibly avoid it, do not go to war when the Democrats control either the executive branch or the legislative branch.
—Interview, *Right Wing News, 6-03*

Q: Do you think liberals were bummed out about Al-Zarqawi getting blown up?

A: Yes, well, naturally they were bummed out, because that got al Qaeda mad at us, and we had been getting along so beautifully until then.
—Interview, *New York Observer, 7-3-06*

FORTUNATELY for liberals, the Iraqis executed Saddam Hussein the exact same week that former President Ford died, so it didn't seem strange that Nancy Pelosi's flag was at half-staff. —"The Democratic Party: A Vast Sleeper Cell," 1-3-07

LIBERALS always want to attack whatever country we're not attacking at that moment. —*Hannity & Colmes, 7-6-06*

NOT exactly smashing stereotypes of liberals as mincing pantywaists, the Left's entire contribution to the war effort thus far has been to whine. —"The Eunuchs Are Whining," 11-1-01

DURING my recent book tour, I resisted the persistent, illiterate request that I name traitors. With a great deal of charity—and suspension of disbelief—I was willing to concede that many liberals were merely fatuous idiots. —"Here's a Traitor!," 9-18-03

IT was not lost on Osama bin Laden that it only took eighteen dead in Somalia for the Great Satan to pull out. It should not be lost on Americans that this is what the Democrats are again demanding we do in Iraq. —"How to Lose a War," 9-11-03

VIETNAM is the Left's favorite war because America lost. —*Treason, p. 125*

DEMOCRATS love taking the nation to war, they just have a phobia about winning. As a consequence, the world's greatest superpower seems to get involved in "unwinnable wars" only when a Democrat is president. —Interview, FrontPage Magazine, 12-23-03

YES, we can avoid war. The way to avoid war is to surrender, and that has been the consistent policy for fifty years of the Democratic Party. —*Hannity & Colmes,* 10-11-06

[T]HE vast majority of liberals are not intentionally sabotaging the nation. In fact, I don't think as many as 20 percent give a damn about the nation. That 20 percent, of course, deeply hates America. —*How to Talk to a Liberal (If You Must), p. 16*

LIBERALS don't mind discussing who is more patriotic if patriotism is defined

as redistributing income and vetoing the Pledge of Allegiance. Only if patriotism is defined as supporting America do they get testy and drone on about "McCarthyism."
—*Treason*, p. 6

ASSUMING against all logic and reason that the Democrats have some serious objection to the war in Iraq, perhaps they could tell us which part of the war on terrorism they do support. That would be easier than rattling off the long list of counterterrorism measures they vehemently oppose.
—"What Part of the War on Terrorism Do They Support?," 8-23-06

[LIBERALS] are either traitors or idiots, and on the matter of America's self-preservation, the difference is irrelevant.
—*Treason*, p. 16

LIBERALS have a preternatural gift for striking a position on the side of treason. You could be talking about Scrabble and they would instantly leap to the anti-American position. —*Treason*, p. 1

DEMOCRATS long to see American mothers weeping for their sons lost in a foreign war, but only if the mission serves absolutely no national security objectives of the United States. If we are building a democracy in a country while also making America safer—such as in Iraq—Democrats oppose it with every fiber of their being. —**"I Did Not Have Sex with That Nomad, Osama Bin Laden," 9-27-06**

[**SENATOR** Patty Murray] told a group of schoolchildren that . . . Osama was beloved because—I quote—"he's been out in the countries for decades building schools, building roads, building infrastructure, building day care facilities, building health care facilities, and people are extremely grateful. He's made their lives better. We have not done that." Yes, bin Laden was building day care facilities for all the working women struggling with career and family under the Taliban. It was like an April Fools' Day hoax. Murray simply assumed the whole NOW agenda was on Osama's program: self-esteem, "infrastructure," battered women's shelters, aromatherapy, the whole nine yards. —*Treason*, p. 253

[**DEMOCRATS**] fill the airwaves with treason, but when called to vote on withdrawing troops, disavow their own public statements. These people are not only traitors, they are gutless traitors. —**"New Idea for Abortion Party: Aid the Enemy,"** 11-23-05

THE nation had been attacked on its own shores, women widowed, children orphaned, thousands of our fellow countrymen killed. Liberals saw this as an occasion to ask, Why do they hate us? —*Treason*, p. 229

HERE the country had finally given liberals a war against fundamentalism and they didn't want to fight it. They would have, except it would put them on the same side as the United States. —*Slander*, p. 5

LIBERALS react to the American flag like Linda Blair did to holy water in **The Exorcist.** —*Treason*, p. 246

PERHAPS we could get Djibouti to like us if we legalized clitorectomies for little girls. America is fighting for its survival and the Democrats are obsessing over why barbarians hate us. —"Why We Hate Them," 9-26-02

THE Left's anti-Americanism is intrinsic to their entire worldview. Liberals promote the rights of Islamic fanatics for the same reason they promote the rights of adulterers, pornographers, abortionists, criminals, and Communists. They instinctively root for anarchy against civilization. The inevitable logic of the liberal position is to be for treason. —*Treason*, p. 292

DEMOCRATS are always hawks in the off-season. —*Treason*, p. 219

LIBERAL RELIGION: AMERICAN IDOLATRY

Liberalism is the sneaky religion that dare not speak its name. We believe in God; liberals believe they **are** God—and they've got the beachfront homes and offshore tax accounts to prove it.

They hate the militant idea in Genesis that we are different from the beasts because we are in God's image. That fact sets us apart singularly, qualitatively, ineluctably from the animals over which we have been given dominion. We carry forward God's story, allowing Him to act through us. There is no purpose to this world without us. That is the first principle of the Bible, the core of what we believe. Once you deny that we alone are in God's image, you have denied everything.

Liberals are animists. They believe we are part of nature—and a not very attractive part. They believe our consciousness cannot be distinguished from lower beasts'. With smoke and mirrors and a sleight of hand with the fossil record, they claim to have discovered a trail from all of us to the lower beasts, proving our ancestral relationship to a worm. Satisfied that they have proved we are no different from the beasts, liberals set to work promoting abortion for inconvenient babies, euthanasia for inconvenient old people, and chemical explanations for evil.

The affirmation of our distinctive humanity is intolerable for liberals. They reject the idea that humans are capable of acting on God's injunction to tinker with our universe or that human creativity is capable of putting more food on the table. They worship no God except themselves. People who worship humanity tend to make lots of bad ethical judgments, such as renaming state-sponsored infanticide "choice." Their religion is a denial of life. It's a denial of us, who are the end of God's creation.

The fanaticism of their refusal to believe the biblical vision of the universe is in direct proportion to the crumbling of the evidence for their own vision. Anything that throws any doubt on the claims of Darwinism is derided as insane and immediately ruled out of order. The more strenuous their shouting, the darker the motive concealed.

Darwin's theory is the hoax of the century. It is the religious belief that must be put into children's heads as early as possible. Everything evil flows from the big lie of evolution. It is all part of the anti-Christian denial of man's soul that began to gather force in the late nineteenth century, erupting in the next century in Nazi fury and Stalinist gulags. Nothing is true, everything is relative, worship rivers and kill babies. The nihilistic religion of Darwinism is even more implacable than the other religion we must abolish: Islam.

ON the seventh day, God rested and liberals schemed. —*Godless*, p. 1

GODLESS examines a set of beliefs known as "liberalism." It is the doctrine that prompts otherwise seemingly sane people to propose teaching children how to masturbate, allowing gays to marry, releasing murderers from prison, and teaching children that they share a common ancestor with the earthworm. (They haven't yet found the common ancestor, but like O.J., the search continues.) —"My Review of My Book," 6-8-06

WHENEVER liberals all start singing from the same hymnal, they are up to no good. (Or since we're talking about American liberals here, maybe I should say, "When they all start reading from the same Koran.") —"Vegan Computer Geeks for Dean," 12-12-03

MATTHEWS: You mean Martin Luther King, who was out there working the religious issue on civil rights, using his cloth, was a godless man?

COULTER: Right. Isn't that curious that you have to go back fifty years to come up with a Democrat who provably believes in God.

—Hardball with Chris Matthews, 7-31-06

LIBERALS do not believe in God because they think they **are** God. And from their experiments in Russia and elsewhere, they would not be a particularly kind and loving one. —Interview, Citizenlink, 10-19-04

FORTUNATELY, the religion of liberalism believes in miracles, so they can hold together completely contradictory beliefs at one time. —*The 700 Club, 7-21-06*

LIBERALS do go crazy at every mention of God, certainly in a public school—including voluntary prayers at football games. But I note that they have a very heightened interest that the terrorists at Guantánamo be free to practice their religion. —*The Phil Donahue Show, 7-18-02*

THE only principle Kwanzaa promotes is liberals' unbounded capacity to respect any faith but Christianity. —"Kwanzaa: Holiday from the FBI," 12-27-06

MOST confusing to Democrats, at the time Reagan was doing all of this Bible-reading and consorting with preachers, he hadn't even been accused of cheating on his wife. What kind of angle was he playing? liberals asked themselves. —**"Let's Rewrite One for The Gipper," 6-17-04**

THAT'S the America you live in! A country founded on a compact with God, forged from the idea that all men are endowed by their Creator with certain unalienable rights, is now a country where taxpayers can be forced to subsidize "artistic" exhibits of aborted fetuses. But don't start thinking about putting up a Ten Commandments display. That's offensive! —**"Thou Shalt Not Commit Religion," 6-29-05**

[**THE** day special prosecutor Patrick Fitzgerald announced his indictments] was going to be Fitzmas Day! (Which is much like Christmas except instead of having her baby in a manger, the woman has a late-term abortion.) —**"Alito Nominated; Democrats Hide from Base," 11-2-05**

IF a Martian landed in America and set out to determine the nation's official state religion, he would have to conclude it is liberalism, while Christianity and Judaism are prohibited by law. And not just in Cambridge, Massachusetts, where it's actually on the books, but throughout the land. —*Godless*, p. 2

[**THE** Democrats' Christian, Jim] Wallis's first remark on the massacre at Virginia Tech last week was to hail the remarkable "diversity" of the victims. True, Cho murdered thirty-two people in cold blood. But at least he achieved diversity! —**"Nuts in the Crosshairs,"** 4-25-07

HANNITY: That was Imam Husham Al-Hussainy of Dearborn, Michigan's Karbalaa Islamic Education Center giving the invocation at a Democratic National Committee's winter meeting. . . .

COULTER: I was just so thrilled to hear that there was prayer! . . . Once they found out that it was a Hezbollah-supporting, Israel-hating imam, they were fine with it. . . .

COLMES: Let me go through this. Stop me when you think this is something a

Christian wouldn't say. "Thank you for making us a great nation." You got a problem with that?

COULTER: Are we going to do this line by line?

COLMES: ... "Moses, Abraham, Muhammad." You got a problem with that?

COULTER: Yes, a Christian wouldn't say that part about Muhammad. ...

COLMES: ... "guide us to the right path, the path of the people you bless, not the people you doom." Do you agree with that?

COULTER: Can you get to the Jew-killing part?

—*Hannity & Colmes*, 2-6-07

HOWARD Dean left the Episcopal Church—which is barely even a church—because his church, in Montpelier, Vermont, would not cede land for the bike path. Environmentally friendly exercise was more important than tending to the human soul. That's all you need to know about the Democrats. Blessed be the peacemakers who create a diverse, nonsexist working environment in paperless offices. —*Godless*, p. 5

EVEN Jimmy Carter, the Democrats' idea of an evangelical Christian, has allowed that "I don't believe that Christ would approve of abortions." (Though Carter added that Christ would approve of abortion if "the mother's life or health was seriously endangered or the pregnancy resulted from rape or incest"—or if Jesus really, really needed the feminists to vote for him.) —"Abortion Stops a Bleeding Heart," 1-25-06

WHILE secularists are constantly comparing conservative Christians to Nazis, somehow it's always the godless doing the genocides. —*Godless*, p. 281

WITH Darwin as their god, everything is just a matter of personal preference. For [Peter] Singer, the utilitarian ethic is based on "quality of life" and prevention of suffering of living things smart enough to teach at Princeton. For Hitler, it was increasing the population of "Aryans." For liberals, the utilitarian ethic is equality of outcome—which they will enforce with fascistic zeal through confiscatory taxation, abortion on demand, racial quotas, gender-norming strength tests, and "everybody gets an 'A' and a blue ribbon."—*Godless*, p. 280

THE Ninth Circuit held that a school can prohibit a student from exercising his First Amendment rights by wearing a T-shirt that said "Homosexuality Is Shameful." Even the Left's pretend-adoration of "free speech" (meaning: treason and pornography) must give way to speech that is contrary to the tenets of the church of liberalism on the sacred grounds of a government school. —"Hey You, Browsing *Godless*—Buy the Book or Get Out!," 6-7-06

[Y]OU must remember that liberals have other sacraments, too—such as polymorphous perversity and putting harmless businessmen in jail. —Interview, News-Max, 7-06

LIBERALS hate religion because politics is a religion substitute for liberals and they can't stand the competition. —*Slander,* p. 194

IF there were a modern Spanish Inquisition in America today, it wouldn't be Bob Jones rounding up Catholics. It would be liberals rounding up right-wingers and putting them on trial for hate crimes. The liberal Torquemadas would be smug and angry and self-righteous. And when they were done, they would proudly announce they had finally banished intolerance. —*Slander,* p. 196

I NOTICE that Howard Dean doesn't give any examples [of Bush being evil]. This is a party that supports killing, lying, adultery, thievery, envy. . . . And they're talking about evil? I think you guys might want to go back to "stupid." —*Hannity & Colmes,* 2-28-05

LIBERALS IN ALPHABETICAL ORDER, OR WHY I SOMETIMES WAVER ON ABORTION

Luxuriating in the warmth of mainstream media admiration, liberal saints get crazier and crazier. They're "beloved," we're "divisive." I only wish more liberals could get famous so we could laugh at them, too.

Here are some quick ones from interviews to get you started:

KOFI Annan: That guy? Isn't he on the ground fighting with Hezbollah?

Katie Couric: The affable Eva Braun of **evening** TV.

Joe Wilson: You mean Valerie Plame's clueless hubby? Whatever happened to that moron?
Dan Rather: Reports of his contrition are greatly exaggerated.
Cynthia McKinney: One of the most intelligent Democrats in the country.
—Interview, *Baltimore Sun,* published in "What I Did on My Summer Vacation," 8-2-06

CINDY Sheehan: The Dennis Rodman of the peace movement.
Joe Wilson: World's most intensely private exhibitionist.
Michael Moore: Rumors of his depth are greatly exaggerated.
John Murtha: The reason soldiers invented "fragging."
Alec Baldwin: Our main source of so-called "greenhouse gases."
—Interview, *Right Wing News,* 6-06

[Madeleine Albright]
APPARENTLY, liberals believe [Condoleezza] Rice compares unfavorably to Madeleine Albright, whose principal accomplishment before becoming secretary of state was managing to attain the age of sixty without realizing she was Jewish. That was raw competence. —"It's Dr. Rice, Not Dr. Dre," 12-1-04

[Yasser Arafat]
YOU only fully appreciate what a despicable man Yasser Arafat is when you watch him retailing lie after lie and think to yourself, **This guy is as bad as Clinton!** —*Treason*, p. 292

[Michael Bloomberg]
BLOOMBERG would only crack down on illegal immigrants if he caught them smoking. —*Treason*, p. 273

[Robert Byrd]
SENATOR Robert Byrd, who was named after a bridge in West Virginia, viciously attacked Treasury Secretary Paul O'Neill for having made a success of himself. Claiming

to speak for worthless layabouts, Byrd snippily informed O'Neill, "They're not CEOs of multibillion-dollar corporations. . . . In time of need, they come to us, the people come to us." Evidently what the people in need are asking for is a **lot** of federal projects named after Senator Byrd. —**"The Robert C. Byrd Bridge to Poverty," 2-14-02**

[Jimmy Carter]
JUDGING from his life's work to date, Carter's definition of a good idea is "an idea likely to hurt America and/or help its enemies." —**"So Three Muslims Walk into a Port," 2-20-06**

[Katie Couric]
IN terms of ratings, Katie's take on the day's events is now running seventh in a field of three, behind Brian Williams at NBC, Charles Gibson at ABC, a cooking show, two home shopping programs, and reruns of **What's Happening!** In other words, Katie Couric has turned the once dominant **CBS Evening News** into the TV equivalent of Air America Radio. —*Godless* **(paperback), p. 289**

[Alan Dershowitz]

DERSHOWITZ has also offered to defend Osama bin Laden in court, saying it would be "an act of high patriotism." It's kind of too bad there isn't going to be a trial. Having Dershowitz defend him could be Osama's only shot at not being the least popular person in the courtroom. —"Mothers Against Box Cutters Speak Out," 10-18-01

[Michael Dukakis]

DUKAKIS didn't even have someone on his staff to warn him, **Just in case you ever think about running for president, sir, you might want to tone down your gushing about furloughs for first-degree murderers.** —*Godless*, p. 71

[John Edwards]

I WAS going to have a few comments on the other Democratic presidential candidate John Edwards, but it turns out you have to go into rehab if you use the word "faggot." —Speech, CPAC, 3-2-07

I WOULDN'T insult gays by comparing them to John Edwards. That would be mean. But about the same time, you know, Bill Maher was not joking saying he wished Dick Cheney had been killed in a terrorist attack. So I've learned my lesson. If I'm going to say anything about John Edwards in the future, I'll just wish he had been killed in a terrorist assassination plot. —*Good Morning America*, 6-25-07

[Al Franken]
AL Franken: Arrogant, ill-mannered, mean-spirited, froglike lying bitch. And those are his good points. —Interview, *Human Events*, 6-29-06

[Al Gore]
GORE always comes out swinging just as an issue is about to go south. He's the stereotypical white guy always clapping on the wrong beat. He grew a beard—just in time for an attack on the nation by fundamentalist Muslims. . . . Gore even went out and got really fat—just before America officially gave up carbs. This guy is always leaping into the mosh pit at the precise moment the crowd parts. —"This Is History Calling—Quick, Get Me a Rewrite!," 6-3-04

[John Kerry and Wesley Clark]
KERRY and Clark now represent the two major wings of the Democratic Party—the Kennedy wing and the Clinton wing. One drowns you after the extramarital affair; the other one calls you a stalker. —"In Search of the Better 'Phony American,'" 1-22-04

[Teresa Heinz Kerry]
TERESA Heinz: the not-so-affable Eva Perón of American politics. —"2004: Highlights and Lowlifes," 12-29-06

[C. Everett Koop]
[W]ITH each more insane statement, Koop was hailed in the media for speaking truth to power. It almost got to the point where Dr. Koop's distinctive look—the gay Amish Navy guy in the Village People—seemed more sane than the things he was saying about AIDS. —*Godless*, p. 179

[Dennis Kucinich]
DENNIS Kucinich did his tax return this week, and under "occupation" he wrote "Jay Leno punch line." —"AFL-CIO Motto: Kick Me Again," 2-26-04

[Joe Lieberman]
JOE Lieberman: A member of the World's Smallest Group: Orthodox Jews for Partial-Birth Abortion. —**"The Hand-Wringing Hamlet of Hartford,"** 8-11-00

[Michael Moore]
MOORE keeps whining about all the right-wing hit groups out to get him. Granted he's a large target (or what's known in baseball as a "fat pitch"). But conservatives are frankly relieved we finally have a liberal who tells the truth about what he thinks of America. —**"Saddam in Custody—Moore, Soros, Dean Still at Large,"** 6-30-04

YOU would think, with all the money Michael Moore is paid, you could afford soap and water. —**Interview,** *New York Observer,* 9-13-04

[B. Hussein Obama]
IN announcing his candidacy last week, Obama confirmed that he believes in "the basic decency of the American people." And let the chips fall where they may! . . . He took a strong stand against the antihope

crowd, saying, "There are those who don't believe in talking about hope." Take that, Hillary! —"Jonathan Livingston Obama," 2-14-07

[Nancy Pelosi]

Q: Even though she is an opponent, as a woman do you think there is any benefit to Nancy Pelosi becoming House speaker?

A: Yes, it shows people the foolishness of putting liberal women in positions of authority. Oops, I've done it again! —Interview, *The Jewish Press*, 3-07

[Pat Robertson]

Q: Your characterization of liberals paints them as extremists. But with people like Pat Robertson telling us how God keeps telling him who He's angry at, isn't it fair to say that there are extremists on both sides?

A: Pat Robertson opposes capital punishment, opposed the impeachment of Bill Clinton, and supports trade with China, just for starters. Seems like a pretty

mixed bag to me. So what makes you call him extreme? That he believes he has dialogue with the Lord? Do liberals now call anyone who thinks this an "extremist"?
—"Top Secret Interview Exposed!," *New York Post*, 7-5-06

[Cindy Sheehan]
WHAT [Mel Gibson] says blind drunk is what Cindy Sheehan says stone cold sober. —*Hannity & Colmes*, 8-2-06

CALL me old-fashioned, but a grief-stricken war mother shouldn't have her own full-time PR flack. After your third profile on **Entertainment Tonight**, you're no longer a grieving mom; you're a C-list celebrity trolling for a book deal or a reality show. —"Cindy Sheehan: Commander in Grief," 8-17-05

THE only sort of authority Cindy Sheehan has is the uncanny ability to demonstrate, by example, what body types should avoid wearing shorts in public. —*Godless*, p. 128

[Valerie Plame Wilson]
[T]HE only person who was undercover in the [Valerie] Plame household was Joe Wilson—under cover of his wife's skirt, that is.
—*Godless*, p. 126

[Joe Wilson]
INCIDENTALLY, if Wilson believed his own Walter Mitty fantasy about his wife being a covert spy—so secret that his entire family could be killed if her identity were revealed—maybe he should have thought twice before writing an op-ed for the **New York Times** calling the president a liar based on information acquired solely because his wife works at the CIA.
—*Godless*, p. 123

ONE could write a book about what Joe Wilson doesn't know about Africa. In fact, I'm pretty sure someone did: Joe Wilson.
—"Mission Implausible," 7-13-05

LIBERAL TACTICS: DISTORTION, DISSEMBLING, DECEPTION—AND THE REST IS JUST RUN-OF-THE-MILL TREASON

The liberals' typical response to a point of blinding clarity is a look of shocked perplexity. They are fiendishly bright in a certain way, but also moronic because they can't see obvious truths. Liberals can study issues one by one and never see a theme emerging. But they're very sneaky.

THIS is the essence of the modern Democratic Party, polished to perfection by Bill Clinton: They are willing to insult the intelligence of 49 percent of the people if they think they can fool 51 percent of the people. —"In Desperate Move, Kerry Adopts Puppy," 7-7-04

AS with all liberal behavior tropes, you could tell what they were up to by what they accused conservatives of. Liberals can't help projecting their own malevolence onto others. —*Treason,* p. 200

Q: A number of folks have criticized you for generalizing about liberals. Is this a fair criticism?

A: In other words, we can't recognize liberals as a group! They should be allowed to do as they please without anyone being able to talk about them. If we couldn't "generalize" about liberals, your question would make no sense. I simply could ask, "What do you mean by 'liberal'?"
—Interview, *Insight* magazine, 9-16-03

[E]VEN when relentlessly destroying people, liberals must pretend to be the ones who are oppressed. All liberals of a certain age claim to have marched with Dr. Martin Luther King and to have been on Nixon's "enemies list," as if every liberal alive during the Nixon administration narrowly escaped the concentration camp. —*Treason*, p. 199

ONE starts to wonder if there are any life-long Democrats, since all the Democrats you meet claim to be "former Republicans" who left the party in disgust. —**"Another Damascus Road Conversion," 8-8-00**

IN a country of almost 300 million people, liberals get seven men to issue an opinion from the Supreme Court and they want the rest of us to shut up about abortion forevermore. But before going to war to eliminate a potential nuclear threat, we need to convince every last American that war is necessary. —*Treason*, p. 220

LIKE everything liberals oppose but don't have a good argument against, all reasonable national security measures are called "unconstitutional." Whenever liberals are losing on substance, they pretend to be upset about process. —**"Liberalism and Terrorism: Different Stages of Same Disease," 7-4-02**

WHEN contemplating a shield that would protect America from incoming missiles, Democrats suddenly became hardheaded fiscal conservatives. . . . These people believe federally funded art therapy for the homeless will pay for itself. That you can take to the bank. But a shield to repel incoming nuclear missiles from American soil, they said, was too expensive and wouldn't work. —*Treason,* p. 162

LIKE all propagandists, liberals create mythical enemies to justify their own viciousness and advance their agenda.—*Slander,* p. 166

I'M getting a little insulted that no Democratic prosecutor has indicted me. Liberals bring trumped-up criminal charges against all the most dangerous conservatives. Why not me?—"Why Can't I Get Arrested?," 12-14-05

[W]HEN conservatives have a position, they write a book, they make an argument. With liberals it's just screaming, hysteria, chaos. —*Hannity & Colmes,* 11-4-05

HISTORY is an endless process of liberal brainwashing. —*Treason*, p. 95

EVEN though liberals make wild professions of how they respect women, they really believe women should be barefoot, pregnant, and in the kitchen. And when they hear a woman who has an opinion, their response is "She's angry! She rants!" This is just liberal sexism. —Interview, Salon, 7-25-03

Democrat **MARY ANNE MARSH:** The fact that Ann's book is number one is just further proof that the only person making money off a book that exploits 9/11 and religion for political purposes is Ann Coulter, and I think that leaves some people—

COULTER: I'm a little tired of liberals exploiting my book to get on TV and sell newspapers.
—*Hannity & Colmes*, 6-15-06

LIKE Oprah during Sweeps Week, liberals have come to rely exclusively on people with sad stories to improve their Q Score.

They've become the Lifetime Television network of political parties. —*Godless*, p. 101

TURN on talk radio right now and you'll hear some liberal caller claiming to be a lifelong Republican scandalized by the Bush tax cuts—or some other policy that has been a mainstay of the Republican Party for at least a century. The callers are always teachers. (No wonder our kids aren't learning—their teachers are always on the phone with talk-radio shows pretending to be Republicans.) —"The Devil Is Out of Details," 5-5-05

LIKE callers to talk radio claiming to be Republicans angry with Republicans, liberals love to pretend public opinion is always in the process of shifting in their direction. —"Poll: Most Americans Love Coulter Columns!," 3-22-06

THE moment you concede some small point to liberals, they go to work building an enormous elaborate edifice on top of the first lie. —*Treason*, p. 74

EXTEND an olive branch to Democrats and they'll smack the living daylights out of you with it—while hugging the tree, naturally. —*How to Talk to a Liberal (If You Must),* p. 13

McCARTHYISM:
CALLING COMMUNISTS
"COMMUNISTS"

The loyal Democrats of this nation no longer have a party. —JOE MCCARTHY

Gloria Steinem said, "When I was in college it was the McCarthy era and that made me a Marxist." When I was in college it was the feminist era, and that made me a Mc-Carthyite.

After Alger Hiss, China, and the Rosenbergs, there was considerably more reason for Joe McCarthy to investigate the State Department than there ever was for Patrick Fitzgerald to investigate Lewis Libby.

The myth of "McCarthyism" arose because only one side cared. The anti-Communism of sensible Americans disproportionately affected teeny, tiny groups of people with enormous influence on the culture: New York intellectuals and Hollywood writers. The only time Hollywood doesn't consider the bottom line is on their pro bono movies about Southern racism and "McCarthyism." There have been a hundred movies about Southern racism and two hundred about McCarthyism. They always lose money. It's as if the studios think they are going to get course credit for making these movies.

So we get weeping martyrdom stories about someone's uncle who made rewrite notes on a film project and then was forced to relinquish the rewrite to another writer. We're shocked by man's inhumanity to man upon hearing of screenwriters who had to move to a less desirable section of Bel-Air. Who's going to make a movie about some unknown Pole—one of thousands—who got a bullet through the head during a Soviet crackdown in Poland?

In one famous case from the eighties, the Soviets brutally murdered the charismatic Catholic priest Jerzy Popieluszko, who had spoken out against the Communist regime in Poland, urging resistance and inspiring Solidarity. After arrests and "car accidents" failed to stop him, he was brutally beaten and murdered by three Security police officers in 1984 and his body dumped in Vistula Water Reservoir.

Someone finally did make a movie about Popieluszko in 1988. The movie bravely gave both sides: the side of the anti-Communist priest and the side of his Communist murderers. How about a movie showing Hitler's side as well as the Jews' side of the story? Who would make such a movie?

Liberals were willing to stay in on weekends to prove their version of history on McCarthy. But so am I.

IF the Internet, talk radio, and Fox News had been around in McCarthy's day, my book wouldn't be the first time most people would be hearing the truth about "McCarthyism."—Interview, *Right Wing News,* 6-03

LOST amid all the mandatory condemnations of Joe McCarthy's name—he gave anti-Communism a bad name, did a disservice to the cause, was an unnecessary distraction—the little detail about his being right always seems to get lost. —*Treason*, p. 71

"MCCARTHYISM" means pointing out positions taken by liberals that are unpopular with the American people. —*Treason*, p. 4

IT breaks my heart to think of what Joe McCarthy could have done if he had had LexisNexis and Google. —*Booknotes*, 8-11-02

[T]O appreciate how the myth of "McCarthyism" was concocted, consider how liberals portray events happening right before our eyes. People who assure us McCarthy presided over a reign of terror also describe Ken Starr's plodding, meticulous investigation as a reign of terror. And they say that when we're watching. Imagine what they'll say when the generation that knows the truth is gone. —*Treason*, p. 100

CONSERVATIVES have moved on from the Clintons. I wrote my book on Bill

Clinton, what, four, five years ago. I have written two books since then. [Liberals] won't stop. They will never, ever give up— Sidney Blumenthal with his 900-page book; Hillary Clinton with her book that gets more coverage than the 9/11 attack; monuments, museums to Bill Clinton. They won't quit. And at some point conservatives just say, okay, fine, fine. If it means that much to you, yes, Clinton was a fine president. Fine. We just don't want to argue with you anymore. And that was essentially what happened to Joe McCarthy.
—*Scarborough Country*, 6-25-03

[H]AVING ceded the lie of "McCarthyism," now no one is allowed to call liberals unpatriotic. Liberals relentlessly attack their own country, but we can't call them traitors, which they manifestly are, because that would be "McCarthyism," which never existed. —*Treason*, p. 75

Q: Richard Nixon served on the House Committee on Un-American Activities. How do you rate his anti-Communist congressional work as compared to that of Senator McCarthy? Who accomplished more?

A: Well, Nixon broke the whole case on Alger Hiss, an act of courage for which Americans must be eternally grateful. (He was never forgiven for it either, of course.) McCarthy was a crucial closer, the mop-up guy, absolutely essential as well. It's like comparing Mike Mussina to Mariano Rivera.
—Interview, American Enterprise Institute, 2004

[T]HERE'S a reason "Communist" now sounds about as threatening as "monarchist"—and it's not because of intrepid **New York Times** editorials denouncing McCarthy and praising Harvard-educated Soviet spies. McCarthy made it a disgrace to be a Communist. —*Treason,* p. 33

PORTRAITS of Kathy Boudin, Che Guevara, Ted Bundy, and Joe Stalin are more nuanced than portraits of McCarthy.
—Interview, FrontPage Magazine, 1-12-04

ETHICAL dilemma: Would you write a book to set the record straight on Joseph McCarthy knowing that it might give rise to yet another lame George Clooney movie? —"Danny Ocean Defends the Rather Network," 11-10-05

JOE McCarthy was an American hero vilified by the Left because he was on to them. As Hubert Humphrey admitted at the time, "McCarthy's real threat to democracy is the fact that he has immobilized the liberal movement." —Interview, *Insight* magazine, 9-16-03

ALGER Hiss is the epitome of liberalism: long on Ivy League credentials, short on character. —Interview, *Insight* magazine, 9-16-03

OWEN Lattimore surely had closer ties to agents of Joseph Stalin than right-wingers do to Richard Mellon Scaife.—*Treason*, p. 89

MCCARTHY is sniffed at for not playing by Marquis of Queensberry Rules—rules of engagement demanded only of Republicans. Well, without McCarthy, Republicans might be congratulating themselves on their excellent behavior from the gulag right now. —*Treason*, p. 71

I WROTE my book, I made my case, and people decided not to argue with me [about Joe McCarthy] on the merits. So now I guess we're back to fact-free invective against McCarthy. —Interview, FrontPage Magazine, 1-12-04

THE principal result of being called a Soviet spy by McCarthy was you got to teach at Harvard. —*Treason*, p. 92

SEDITION always held a strong attraction for Ivy League types with three names, like John Stewart Service, Harry Dexter White, George Catlett Marshall, and William Sloane Coffin. It was a quirky thing about WASPs. They took perverse pride in harboring the periodic traitor. —*Treason*, p. 61

YOU can produce the DNA evidence. You can produce the decrypted Soviet cables to their spies in America and [liberals] will not give up. They just act like they missed that day's news when the Venona decrypts were released and go right back to talking about the innocent victims of McCarthyism. —*Scarborough Country*, 6-25-03

Q: Whittaker Chambers was extremely critical of Senator McCarthy. . . . What do you make of Mr. Chambers's position on Senator McCarthy?

A: Let's face it, Chambers was a bit of a pessimist and he was not known for his good judgment. He did join the Communist Party, after all. And even after he switched, he thought Communism would win. In any event, it's irrelevant what Chambers thought of McCarthy. John McCain is a war hero—and he attacks the Swift Boat veterans. I take it you're not arguing that McCain's opposition proves the Swifties are wrong either in substance or tactics. McCarthy had to do what he had to do. He may not have had sufficient forces to do battle with the whole Soviet empire, but he

bought America time, until Ronald Reagan could come in and save the world.
—Interview, American Enterprise Institute, 2004

"**MCCARTHYISM**" is one of the markers on the left's Via Dolorosa. It is their slavery, their Gulag, their potato famine. Otherwise, liberals would just be geeks from Manhattan and Hollywood. —*Treason*, p. 75

MAYBE it would have been better if McCarthy had been more measured in his rhetoric. And maybe it would have been better if Ken Starr had the savoir faire of Cary Grant and if Linda Tripp looked like Gwyneth Paltrow, and Monica—No, Monica was perfect. But were there Soviet spies in the State Department? —*Treason*, p. 123

EVEN people who know better are constantly being forced to declaim McCarthy a very bad man just so liberals will leave them alone. It is the code word that must be uttered to gain acceptance into the halls of establishmentarian opinion. —*Treason*, p. 55

FOR fifty years Hollywood drama queens have churned out plays, movies, TV shows, books, poems, allegories, museum exhibits, personal testimonials, dioramas, interpretive dances, wood carvings, cave paintings, needlepoint wall hangings, and scatological limericks about their victimization at the hands of a brute named Joe McCarthy. . . . But half a century of mythmaking later, one little book comes out and gives the contrary view—and Hollywood thinks it's Treblinka.
—"Danny Ocean Defends the Rather Network," 11-10-05

DESPITE the left's creation of a myth to defeat legitimate charges of treason, McCarthy had so badly stigmatized Communism, his victory survived him. In his brief fiery ride across the landscape, Joe McCarthy bought America another thirty years. For this he sacrificed his life, his reputation, his name. The left cut down a brave man, but not before the American people heard the truth. —*Treason*, p. 71

HAVING been proved wrong on their primary charge against Joe McCarthy, that,

"Oh, he was imagining some crazy Communist conspiracy to infiltrate the government"—that was the big point—having been proved wrong on that, I would think that liberals would have a little less credibility on the rest of their charges. But, in fact . . . what most people would say [is] "Well, yes, of course, he was right, but he didn't have to be so mean." —*Scarborough Country,* 6-25-03

Q: Why do you think Joe McCarthy has gotten a bad rap?

A: I know he got a bad rap because there are no monuments to Joe McCarthy.
—Interview, *Right Wing News,* 6-03

THE MILITARY—THEIR PET PEEVE: KEEPING GEORGE CLOONEY SAFE

Despite the impression left by the TV generals and Democratic politicians, which suggests that the words "I wore the uniform" invariably precede a call to surrender, liberals might want to steer clear of demanding that the nation defer to the views of the military.

The vast majority of people in the military voted for George Bush. And they are getting a little irritated with the liberal antiwar crowd bragging about their war records in order to mau-mau the rest of us. Ever since liberal veterans realized they could score at a **Vanity Fair** party, they have gotten a little too full of themselves. The list of liberal luminaries boasting of wartime service is getting out of control.

According to a **Military Times** survey taken in September 2004, active-duty military personnel preferred President Bush to John Kerry by about 73 percent to 18 percent. Sixty percent describe themselves as Republican, and less than 10 percent call themselves Democrat (the same 10 percent that MSNBC has on its speed dial). Even among veterans, Republicans outnumber Democrats 46 percent to 22 percent.

Jock sniffers for military veterans are very picky about which veterans they respect. When Clinton was their candidate, it was a dirty trick for anyone to mention the war record of the first George Bush or Bob Dole. Howard Dean was nearly the Democratic candidate for president in 2004. What would liberals have done then? Dean spent the Vietnam War skiing in Colorado.

The media were not half as interested in Pat Tillman when he walked away from a million-dollar-a-year contract with the NFL's Arizona Cardinals to join the United States Army as when he died in Afghanistan. Tillman was the first player to leave a career in professional football in order to volunteer for military service since World War II. But the **New York Times** ran a mere three articles on that story. Only after Tillman's death in Afghanistan did the **Times**'s interest in him soar, leading to twenty-four articles leering over his death as a result of friendly fire. Apparently, the story of a patriotic American was only one-eighth as interesting as the story of a dead patriotic American.

The media's obsession with Tillman's death, but not his life, derives from the preposterous idea that to be killed by friendly fire in combat is a horribly inglorious ending—and also that such deaths never happened in wars before Bush. This is absurd. Any soldier in combat runs the risk of being hit by our own side's bullets.

Unlike Max Cleland, Tillman was in an authentic battle against the enemy. Bullets were flying, smoke was billowing, and the enemy was fleeing. His life was no more "wasted" than any other combat death. Friendly-fire casualties have a special poignancy, but it's outrageous for anyone to refer to friendly fire in a combat zone as "fratricide."

Admittedly, it was ham-handed of the Army to fib about it: presumably the officer on the ground made the mistake of trying to spare Tillman's family some small amount of pain by hiding the fact that it was friendly fire that killed Tillman. But the insensate Democratic campaign to imply that friendly fire is a form of incompetence unique to wars fought under George Bush is ludicrous. Tillman was honorable and courageous, and—unlike Max Cleland—he sustained his injuries in combat. His was a genuine, 100 percent, incontrovertible combat death.

The same media that are reverential toward Max Cleland for dropping a grenade on himself in a noncombat situation are now exuberant that Tillman was killed by friendly fire in combat, acting as if they have uncovered a major scandal. It all comes down to what Patton said: "They know no more about military operations than about fornicating, having never been involved in either one."

[W]AR is a bad thing. But once a war starts, it is going to be finished one way or another, and I have a preference for it coming out one way rather than the other. —"Live and Let Spy," 12-21-05

WHEN our troops came under a bloody attack in Somalia in 1993, President Clinton ordered a humiliating retreat— on the advice of John Murtha. . . . And sure enough, perhaps just out of force of habit, Clinton pulled out before finishing. —*Godless*, p. 141

I'M just so happy when you liberals become fiscal conservatives. You don't mind when the government is spending money on photos of bullwhips up men's asses. . . . But the one thing we've got to watch out for is spending on the military. —*Hannity & Colmes*, 5-5-04

WAR ended slavery, fascism, Soviet totalitarianism, but other than that, it has a limited repertoire. [Sheryl] Crow explained that the "best way to solve problems is to not have enemies." War solves that problem too: We won't have any enemies because we're going to kill them. —*Treason*, p. 248

IF Gore had been elected president, right now he would just be finding that last lesbian quadriplegic for the Special Forces team. —"Fall Fashion Preview: Cowboy Boots In, Flip-Flops Out," 10-13-04

SAY, when is the **Times** going to hire generals to review the latest Broadway offerings? I think more people would like to read Tommy Franks's review of **Rent** than Frank Rich's review of a war. —"Dems' Favorite Halloween Costume: Patriot," 10-24-06

IN his acceptance speech at the Democratic National Convention, John Kerry proposed "investing" in Head Start, Early Start, Smart Start, Jump Start, Kick Start— and got a standing ovation. He mentioned the military and you could hear crickets in the convention hall. —*Godless*, p. 152

IF those of us who didn't fight are wimps who don't know the real truth of war, I say,

Fine. Let's allow only combat veterans and active military members to vote. Everybody else shut up—including me and the vast majority of liberals. Kerry, Kerrey, Cleland, Inouye, and Murtha—that's it; they've got five votes. —*Godless*, p. 138

HEY! Wasn't women in the military a great idea until we had a war? —**"Affirmative Action for Osama,"** 10-11-01

AL Gore . . . like [John] Kerry, was in Vietnam just long enough to get photos for his future political campaigns. (Apparently all future Democratic politicians take cameras to war zones.) —**"Ballad of the French Berets,"** 8-18-04

ENRAGINGLY, liberals talk about Vietnam as if it proves something about the use of force generally rather than the Democrats' own bungling incompetence in military affairs. Historical accounts of the Vietnam War are incomprehensible because liberals refuse to admit the failure of their own national security strategy. The only important lesson from the

Vietnam War is this: Democrats lose wars.
—*Treason*, p. 125

DEMOCRATS think they invented war heroes, but being a war hero didn't help Bob Dole. It didn't help George Herbert Walker Bush. It didn't help John McCain. The Democrats didn't invent war heroes. What they invented is the scam of deploying war heroes to argue for surrender. —**"Boobs in the News,"** 2-4-04

JOHN Kerry is the "botched joke" of American politics. For those of you keeping score at home, John Kerry has now called members of the U.S. military (a) stupid, (b) crazy, (c) murderers, (d) rapists, (e) terrorizers of Iraqi women and children. . . . Whatever Karl Rove is paying John Kerry to say stupid things, it's worth every penny. —**"Jihad Is Fun! Vote Democrat!,"** 11-1-06

INSTEAD of relentlessly attacking the military as immature or testosterone-crazed—meaning "braver than me"—liberals might have the good grace to realize they live in a country where big burly men are willing to protect them from bullies. As far as I am aware, the military does not interfere in the fashion industry. They don't have a lot of opinions about Broadway plays or write poetry like Clinton's secretary of defense, William Cohen. Why can't liberals let men defend the country? —*Treason*, p. 243

> # MORALS: GET CHUCK SCHUMER OVER HERE, I DON'T WANT TO HAVE TO EXPLAIN THIS TWICE!

I've been interested in the Democratic Party ever since I read **Lolita.**

I notice that the only time liberals care about child molestation is if a Catholic priest is involved. That's "hypocrisy"—and hypocrisy is the only vice that really steams them. Liberals can never be guilty of hypocrisy no matter how debauched their behavior, because they cheerfully admit that they have no morals. "That wasn't us, that was you guys."

THIS is an age in which the expression "girls gone wild" is becoming a redundancy. —"Lie Down with Strippers, Wake Up with Pleas," 4-19-06

TODAY'S brain twister: Would you rather be O.J.'s girlfriend or Michael Schiavo's fiancée? —"The Emperor's New Robes," 3-30-05

DESPITE the growing media consensus that Catholicism causes sodomy, an alternative view—adopted by the Boy Scouts—is that sodomites cause sodomy. —"Should Gay Priests Adopt?," 3-21-02

IT'S nice to see liberals becoming such big marriage-boosters. Too bad their newfound respect for marriage—an eminently dissolvable agreement, rescindable by either party without cause or notice—is limited to gays and priests. —"Should Gay Priests Adopt?," 3-21-02

[A]CCORDING to the only serious, long-term scientific study of the sexual behavior of Americans ever performed, 75 percent of married men and 85 percent of married women have never been unfaithful. . . . **Never.** And consider that that figure includes couples who are separated or headed toward divorce court. (And further consider that residents of Manhattan and Malibu were included in the category "Americans.") —**"If You Sup with the Devil, Use a Long Spoon," published in 2004,** *How to Talk to a Liberal (If You Must)*

EVERY woman who has had an abortion feels compelled to defend abortion for all women; every man who's ever been at a party with strippers thinks he has to defend all men who watch strippers; and every Democrat who voted for Bill Clinton feels the need to defend duplicity, adultery, lying about adultery, sexual harassment, rape, perjury, obstruction of justice, kicking the can of global Islamofascism down the road for eight years, and so on. —**"Lie Down with Strippers, Wake Up with Pleas," 4-19-06**

IF we make excuses for evil—Hitler was a "madman," a pedophile priest was "weak," or, as philandering actor Ethan Hawke recently advised us, Bill Clinton "suffered from" infidelity—soon we cease being able to distinguish good from evil at all. (I would add to the excuses for evil, "It's just about sex.") —**"Deliver Us from Democrats,"** 4-8-04

FOR liberals, not making moral judgments is the very essence of science. On that theory, Howard Stern should be curing cancer and inventing cold fusion any day now.—*Godless,* p. 180

IF leading scientists believed fetal stem-cell research would prove to be so fruitful in curing Alzheimer's, why is the private money not pouring in hand over fist? Do you realize how many billions a cure for Alzheimer's would be worth, let alone all the other cures some are claiming fetal stem-cell research would lead to? Forget Alzheimer's—do you know how much middle-aged men would pay for a **genuine** baldness cure? Then again, Porsche sales would probably fall off quite a bit if we ever cured baldness. —"Let's Rewrite One for The Gipper!," 6-17-04

[A]FTER two weeks of TV coverage of the Terri Schiavo case, I think we have almost all liberals in America on record saying we can pull the plug on them. Of course, if my only means of entertainment were Air America Radio, Barbra Streisand albums, and reruns of **The West Wing**, I too would be asking, "What kind of quality of life is this?" —"The Emperor's New Robes," 3-30-05

YOU can't grow peanuts on your own land or install a toilet capable of disposing two tissues in one flush because of federal government intervention. But Congress demands a review of the process that goes into a governmental determination to kill an innocent American woman—and that goes too far! —"The Emperor's New Robes," 3-30-05

IN the worldview of a liberal, it is wrong to have sex with a donkey because, absent the animal's consent, it would be rape. (Remember: Whinny means "no"!) . . . How about this: Any person who wants to have sex with an animal should be in a straitjacket? —*Godless*, p. 276

INASMUCH as liberals have no morals, they can sit back and criticize other people for failing to meet the standards that liberals simply renounce. . . . By openly admitting to being philanderers, draft dodgers, liars, weasels, and cowards, liberals avoid ever being hypocrites. —"With Half His Brain Tied Behind His Back," 10-16-03

[On arguments for drug legalization]
THE idea that making an activity legal would reduce its incidence is preposterous. This is exactly like the Clintonian statement about wanting to make abortion "safe, legal and rare." The most effective way to make something "rare" is to make it illegal. —*How to Talk to a Liberal (If You Must)*, p. 312

PEOPLE who say "everybody does it" are announcing nothing more than the implacable fact that **they** do it. —"If You Sup with the Devil, Use a Long Spoon," published in 2004, *How to Talk to a Liberal (If You Must)*

WE live in an America in which soccer moms swoon over Bill Clinton, and Larry Flynt is a cultural icon. . . . Our men are up to the job of protecting us from foreign enemies, but our women are losing the war at home. —*Treason, p. 290*

LIBERALS hate society and want to bring it down to reinforce their sense of invincibility. Secure in the knowledge that their beachfront haciendas will still be standing when the smoke clears, they giddily fiddle with the little people's rules and morals. —*Slander, p. 27*

I HAVEN'T checked with any Harvard Law professors, but I'm pretty sure that, generally, adulterous drunks who drive off bridges and kill girls are prosecuted. Ah, but Teddy Kennedy supports adultery and public drunkenness—so at least you can't call him a hypocrite! That must provide great consolation to Mary Jo Kopechne's parents. —**"With Half His Brain Tied Behind His Back," 10-16-03**

LIKE the Democrats, **Playboy** just wants to liberate women to behave like pigs, have sex without consequences, prance about naked, and abort children. —**"The Viagra Cotillion," 8-15-00**

AMERICAN liberals have used their hegemonic control of televisions, movies, glossy magazines, and newspapers to create a charming world in which women apparently cannot bear to keep their shirts on. —*Treason, p. 289*

MUSLIMS: SANTA CLAUS, THE EASTER BUNNY, AND A MODERATE MUSLIM WALK INTO A BAR . . .

Hey! Good Muslims! Come out, come out, wherever you are!

These Muslims have a more exaggerated sense of pride than prevailed in the Old South. There, at least, duels were confined to matters of love and honor. Although, truth be told, even more pernicious than Muslims are liberals, all of whom are bad.

INASMUCH as liberals are demanding that Americans ritualistically proclaim, "Islam is a religion of peace," Muslims might do their part by not killing people all the

time. —"Beauty Pageants Can Be Murder,"
12-2-02

I THINK we'd all be more interested in looking at [violent passages from the Old Testament] and looking at the life of Moses and what the Old Testament teaches if Jews were flying planes into skyscrapers, shouting "**Allahu akbar,**" slaughtering thousands of innocent Americans. —*Buchanan & Press*, 11-26-02

FINE, we get it. The **New York Times** can rest assured that every last American has now heard the news that not all Muslims are terrorists. That's not the point. Not all Muslims may be terrorists, but all terrorists are Muslims—at least all terrorists capable of assembling a murderous plot against America that leaves 3,000 people dead in under two hours. —"Future Widows of America: Write Your Congressman," 9-28-01

Q: What do you think of the suggestion that putting pressure on Israel to concede to the Arabs would moderate the Middle East?

A: Oh sure, making concessions to the Arabs has never, ever worked in the past, so why not try it again?
—Interview, *The Jewish Press,* 3-07

THE little darlings brandish placards with typical Religion of Peace slogans, such as "Behead Those Who Insult Islam," "Europe, you will pay, extermination is on the way," and "Butcher those who mock Islam." They warn Europe of their own impending 9/11 with signs that say, "Europe: Your 9/11 will come"—which is ironic, because they almost had me convinced the Jews were behind the 9/11 attack. —"Calvin and Hobbes—and Muhammad," 2-8-06

WHY should Islam be subject to presumption of respect because it's a religion? Liberals bar the most benign expressions of religion by little America. Only a religion that is highly correlated with fascistic attacks on the United States demands their respect and protection. —**"Murder for Fun & Prophet," 9-5-02**

IF our enemies aren't "true Muslims," why are the "true Muslims" always so offended on their behalf? —**"Bush Official Caught in Church Dragnet," 10-23-03**

THE ironic thing is, liberals would hate Muslims who practiced only "true Islam." Without the terrorism, Muslims would just be another group of "anti-choice" fanatics. —**"Beauty Pageants Can Be Murder," 12-2-02**

SOMEONE should tell Janet Reno that Islamic fundamentalism is an offshoot of the Branch Davidians. —**"Where's Janet Reno When We Need Her?," 9-20-01**

***NEW* York Times** columnist Thomas Friedman has written that our only choices in response to terrorism are to "become less open as a society" or simply "to live with much higher levels of risk." I have another solution. It's a little something I've worked up— I like to call it "racial profiling." —**Speech, University of Colorado-Boulder, 11-14-03**

TAKING to heart the lesson that violence works, I hereby announce to the world: I am offended by hotel windows that don't open, pilots chattering when the passengers are trying to sleep, and Garfield cartoons. Next time my sleep is disturbed by gibberish about our altitude over Kansas, the National Pilots Emirate embassy is going down. —**"So, Three Muslims Walk into a Port,"** 2-22-06

[I]**T'S** not exactly a scoop that Muslims are engaging in violence. A front-page story would be "Offended Muslims Remain Calm." —**"Muslim Bites Dog,"** 2-15-06

NOBODY around throughout World War II was saying, "Most Germans are peaceful. Most Germans are peaceful. **Mein Kampf** does have some good points." —*Buchanan & Press,* 11-26-02

AS my regular readers know, I've long been skeptical of the "Religion of Peace" moniker for Muslims—for at least 3,000 reasons right off the top of my head. —**"Calvin and Hobbes—and Muhammad,"** 2-8-06

Q: Wouldn't a hunt for "swarthy males" have missed the 1995 bomber of Oklahoma City, the Gulf War veteran, and all-American white male Timothy McVeigh?

A: Ah, the old Timothy McVeigh chestnut. A few years ago, a man was killed with a crossbow in Brooklyn. That doesn't mean New York City cops should be focusing on the problem of crossbow violence.

—Interview, *The Guardian* (U.K.), 5-17-03

[P]ONDER the image of the middle-of-the-road, "centrist" jihadist who could be "recruited" to jihad by reports about abuse at Guantánamo. You know—the kind of guy who just watches Al Jazeera for the sports and hits the "mute" button whenever they start in about the Jews again, already.

Liberals want us to believe such a person exists and that he is perusing newspaper articles about Guantánamo trying to decide whether to finish his coffee and head off to work or to place a backpack filled with dynamite near a preschool.

Note to liberals: That doesn't happen.

—"Losing Their Heads over Gitmo," 6-15-05

Q: You told the **New York Observer** a little more than a year ago that you were hoping to have a fatwa issued against you but hadn't yet succeeded. Any change on that front in the last fourteen months?

A: Alas, no. In addition to being savage, dirty, and violent, Islamic fanatics are apparently also lazy, since they are obviously not reading my stuff.
—Interview, Citizenlink, 10-19-04

RECENTLY, the Religion of Peace suffered a PR setback when Muslims in Nigeria welcomed the Miss World beauty pageant by slaughtering Christians in the street and burning churches to the ground. . . . (Overheard at Miss World contest: "Does this make me look fatwa?") —**"Beauty Pageants Can Be Murder,"** 12-2-02

I THINK a very important distinction here, and I wish more Muslims would observe this, as well, is the difference between speech and ripping out a man's entrails. [Christian leaders] are not killing anyone. They are not hurting anyone. They are simply engaging in speech. —*Buchanan & Press,* 11-26-02

I'M working on a Muslim version of **The Da Vinci Code** in which the prophet is a big phony, he leads a double life, his whole religion is based on a lie, etc., etc. That won't be offensive to anybody, will it? Think I'll have any trouble finding a publisher? A Hollywood production company to buy the movie rights? —Interview, NewsMax, 7-06

THE New York Times called the Spanish election [acquiescing to al Qaeda bombings] "an exercise in healthy democracy." And an ATM withdrawal with a gun to your head is a "routine banking transaction." —"Al Qaeda Barks, the Spanish Fly," 3-17-04

MUSLIMS are the only group who kill because they're angry people have called them violent. —Speech, CPAC, 2-10-06

DONAHUE: [Y]ou take some heavy incoming from [David] Brock's book, which I'm sure you read.

COULTER: I did not read it. I don't know anyone who read it.

DONAHUE: Let me just tell you. He accuses you, among other things, of being an anti-Semite.

COULTER: Maybe that will help me with the Muslims.

—*The Phil Donahue Show,* 7-18-02

OKAY, I made a few jokes. They killed three thousand Americans. I think we're even. —Q &A, CPAC, 2-10-06

THE *NEW YORK TIMES:* DON'T LOOK NOW, BUT THE OLD GRAY LADY IS ON A RESPIRATOR

The lie-by-omission technique has been raised to an art form by the **New York Times**. You simply never hear about whatever doesn't fit the **Times**'s ideological preconceptions. The **Times** also thinks that because there are sophistical arguments to be made, it's their responsibility to roll them out triumphantly.

Of course, consider their constituency. The letters to the editor in the **Times** suggest that almost all their readers are fruit-juice faddists and vegetarians who simply cannot understand why that reckless cowboy in the White House is so determined to keep troops in Iraq when Nancy Pelosi was making so much progress with that nice man in Syria.

In 2006, the **New York Times** revealed a top secret National Security Agency program tracking phone calls to numbers found in Khalid Sheikh Mohammed's cell phone. Experts believe this may have been **almost** as damaging to national security as the revelation that Mr. Valerie Plame was sent on an unpaid junket to Niger by his wife. Also treasonous, which, unlike the crime of engaging in free speech outside an abortion clinic, is a crime specifically defined in the Constitution.

As I see it, the one bargaining chip the **Times** has is this: They could offer to put Pinch Sulzberger in the brig until he coughs up his SAT scores. Sure, those numbers may be confidential. But like the NSA terrorist surveillance program, everybody already knows about them anyway, right? So what's the difference? To paraphrase Tom Brokaw, are people really going to be shocked by the release of documentary evidence that Pinch Sulzberger is mildly retarded?

The public hilarity that will result from

revealing Pinch's SAT scores might finally provoke **Times** shareholders to revolt and appoint some distant cousin to take his place. And for the anti-death-penalty crowd, the sublime pleasure of revealing what a nincompoop this little twerp is would obviate the need to shoot him. He'd have to go crawling off to the mountains like a wounded dog. It's a tough choice, but the **Times** is going to have to tell us the whole story. Otherwise, the NSA is reclassifying Pinch's SAT scores as "classified" and the **Times** will be forced to print them.

THANKS to the **New York Times**, the easiest job in the world right now is "Head of Counterintelligence—Al Qaeda." —"12 Down: Top Secret War Plans, 36 Across: Treason," 6-28-06

THEIR reaction to Zarqawi's death was to lower the U.S. flag at the **Times** building to half-staff. (Ha ha—just kidding! Everybody knows there aren't any American flags at the **New York Times**.) —"*N.Y. Times: Better Dead Than Read*," 7-12-06

MY only regret with Timothy McVeigh is he did not go to the **New York Times** building. —Interview, *New York Observer*, 8-20-02

OF course I regret [saying McVeigh should have gone to the **New York Times** building]. I should have added, "After everyone had left the building except the editors and reporters." —Interview, *Right Wing News*, 6-03

WINNING "Best in Show" was the **Times**'s headline on an article about the Christian missionary shot dead in Lebanon by a Muslim: "Killing Underscores Enmity of Evangelists and Muslims." This is like referring to the enmity between a woman and her rapist. She hates him, he hates her. It's a cycle of violence! Except the funny thing about the Christians is, they still love the Muslims. —"**Beauty Pageants Can Be Murder**," 12-2-02

LIBERALS whose principal argument against Republican after Republican is that they are all idiots should put up or shut up. We want the [SAT] scores of every reporter who ever sneered at the intelligence of Reagan or Bush. Especially Maureen Dowd and Howell Raines. —*Slander,* p. 154

I TEND to always be in favor of there being more speech, more information. And when I say speech, I actually mean speech; unlike the **New York Times**, I don't mean child pornography. —*The O'Reilly Factor,* 5-17-02

THE newspaper that almost missed the war in Iraq because its reporters were in Georgia covering the membership policies of the Augusta National Golf Club has declared another one of President George Bush's judicial nominees as "out of the mainstream." —"The 'Mainstream' Is Located in France," 10-28-03

Q: If President Bush called you today and asked you for your advice on the next moves he should take in our battle with militant Islam, what would you advise?

A: Fire U.S. Transportation Secretary Norman Mineta. Keep excluding the **New York Times** from all exclusive press briefings.
—Interview, FrontPage Magazine,
1-12-04

IN a November 9, 2003, news article, the **New York Times** raised the prospect that "democracy in the Middle East might empower the very forces that the United States opposes, like Islamic fundamentalists in Saudi Arabia and Egypt." Democracy in the United States might have put John Kerry in the White House, too, but you'll notice we didn't abandon the idea.
—"Ever Have One of Those Millennia?,"
5-11-05

AMAZINGLY, no matter how many conservative minorities Bush sends up [for federal judgeships], the **Times** has not been able to find a single one who is "qualified." The **Times** thinks Justice [Janice Rogers] Brown should be the maid and Miguel Estrada the pool boy. —"The 'Mainstream' Is Located in France," 10-30-03

INSTEAD of being a record of history, the **Times** is merely a record of what liberals would like history to be: **The Pentagon in Crisis! A Quagmire in Iraq! Global Warming Is Melting the North Pole! Protests Roil the Augusta National Golf Club!** Publisher Arthur "Pinch" Sulzberger has turned the paper into a sort of bulletin board for Manhattan liberals. —**"How a White Male from Alabama Learned the Craft of Journalism from a Young Reporter Named Jayson Blair," 5-14-03**

WHEN I told a **New York Observer** reporter that my only regret was that Timothy McVeigh didn't hit the **New York Times** building, I knew many would agree with me—but I didn't expect that to include the **New York Times.** And yet, the **Times** is doing everything in its power to help the terrorists launch another attack on New York City. —**"***N.Y. Times:*** **Better Dead Than Read," 7-13-06**

OLD MEDIA: IMAGINE AN OPEN SEWER WITH COUPONS, WANT ADS, AND YOUR HOROSCOPE

In 2002, **Washington Post** reporter Ceci Connolly complained that it was "awkward" for the media after September 11 because "we certainly did not want to seem unpatriotic." Can we ask why seeming unpatriotic was a temptation?

The proposition that the mainstream media (MSM) aren't rabidly anti-American is absurd. They run a Leni Riefenstahl-style media campaign to persuade Americans we're losing in Iraq and must surrender to the jihadists. They might fool some decent Midwesterner into believing in this "alternative patriotism" of theirs, which evidently involves constantly attacking their own country.

But they're talking to me. I know they're traitors. Say, how about the MSM showing aborted fetuses like they show American combat deaths? Murdered unborn babies outnumber brave fallen troops by about 2,000 to 1. Isn't that newsworthy?

Liberals still own 90 percent of the information dissemination in America, but are inconsolable over the death of Old Media's monolithic control. How much control do they want? These people used to become indignant when conservatives attacked the media. But now they won't shut up about the media and act as if the mere existence of Fox News has put them in the midst of a police state.

The MSM keep trying to pawn off their favorite myths to Americans and then blame their "scrappy" competitors when no one cares. They've got the technology, the catchy jingles, the money, and the control. Their only problem is: The dogs don't like it. Liberals seem genuinely mystified that they can't sell John McCain to Republicans. They're perplexed by the lack of riots over the males-only membership rules at the Augusta National Golf Club. But perhaps their most incredible myth is the one about themselves and how objective they are.

Fox News isn't conservative (despite liberals repeating that to themselves over and over again). But it does promote something liberals fear more than anything other than the FBI being able to see the porn sites they've visited: debate. What really distinguishes Fox News is that its prime-time lineup is predicated on conservatives and liberals debating, which regularly results in liberals being trounced.

For obvious reasons, the MSM's primary goal is to prevent debate from ever happening. Their idea of "debate" was in evidence on the April 22, 2007, edition of NBC's **Meet the Press,** in which four media elites bemoaned the failure of new gun-control measures after the Virginia Tech shootings and argued about how the Democrats might be able to slip new gun-control laws past Americans. Not one panelist opposed gun-control laws. Excerpts:

> **TIM RUSSERT:** . . . yet neither party seemed to be very enthusiastic this week . . . about gun control.

JON MEACHAM: No, and I think you saw what the Democrats—there was a lot of kind of deafening silence, in a way, on the gun issue most of the week.

DORIS KEARNS GOODWIN: It seems to me, though, that the Democrats are misreading history when they blame the 2000 election on [anti-]gun-control strength.

DAVID GREGORY: Keeping guns out of the hands of those who are mentally unstable seems like an obvious area to bring in the NRA, to bring in the public policy folks, politicians.

PETE WILLIAMS: Right, well, the Virginia attorney general's office is already looking at whether the Virginia law needs to be changed.

The prospect of open debate with conservatives throws the mainstream media into a hissy fit that rivals an Alec Baldwin phone call to his daughter. Instead, the press prefers to run self-flagellating articles lamenting their failure to attack President Bush with sufficient vigor. They can't even listen to Bush without heckling him. They treat seriously every bizarre conspiracy theory about him to come down the pike. CBS News's Dan Rather was caught using forged documents to try to throw a presidential election against him. What else are they supposed to do? Assassinate him?

Arabs have one propaganda book, **The Protocols of the Elders of Zion.** Liberals have about forty thousand propaganda outlets. In fact, they increasingly resemble the Iraqi insurgents—desperate and violent because they're frustrated that they are losing intellectually.

PRAVDA had certain shortcomings in Soviet days, but at least it was honest enough to admit being a Communist Party newspaper. —Interview, *Il Foglio* (Italy), 10-04

IN case you aren't able to read ACLU press releases for yourself, the Associated Press and the **New York Times** will helpfully restate them for you as important, breaking "news." —"'All the News We Get from the ACLU,'" 4-26-01

LIBERALS defend every manner of pornography and filth on grounds that it's "what the people want." Editors, we are constantly lectured, only "want to sell newspapers." The only material too prurient to let the public read is anything written by a conservative. —*How to Talk to a Liberal (If You Must)*, p. 321

HAVE you ever seen **Citizen Kane**? You know, Kane marries the nightclub singer and then wants to make her a great opera singer. Because he controls all news in America, even though the audience is booing and throwing paper airplanes [at her], the headline on every newspaper is "Susan Alexander Sweeps Chicago!" That is what it's like to be a liberal in America. —Interview, *New York Observer*, 1-10-05

Q: Let's talk a little about how you're portrayed in the media. They don't like you very much. Why?

A: They are instruments of the international Communist conspiracy. —Interview, Citizenlink, 10-19-04

EITHER every single person working in the media today is thoroughly incompetent in every way, or this massive, daily misrepresentation is the result of left-wing bias throughout the media. I'll let you decide which is the most plausible. —*Interview, Baltimore Sun*, 7-30-06

IF I could just mention this—I'm sitting in the Fox studio in L.A. I don't know why there's a copy of **Newsweek** here rather than **Human Events.** But here it is, the new **Newsweek,** describing Ann Coulter as saying 9/11 widows enjoyed their husbands' death. Now, that is simply a lie. That is a lie. If you can't deal with the facts and you refuse to say what the argument is, I think that shows a little lack of confidence in your position, and it certainly shows a complete lack of understanding about how Americans can find out the truth these days. It is not the mainstream media monopoly it was ten years ago. —*Hannity & Colmes*, 6-15-06

MOST politicians would rather face down the Vietcong than be ridiculed by Katie

Couric. It's one thing to be hung upside down and have bamboo shoots stuck under your fingernails. But for the media to accuse you of being against "progress and enlightenment" or call you an "airhead"—well, that makes strong men tremble and weak men liberals. —*Slander,* p. 51

LIBERAL fairness is: They get all major means of news dissemination in America, and conservatives get the **Washington Times,** the editorial page of the **Wall Street Journal,** and Fox News Channel. —*Slander,* p. 59

WHO'S going to give me a TV show? I didn't work for an impeached, disbarred president who was held in contempt by a federal judge. That's what they look for in objective reporters. —Interview, *New York Observer,* 8-20-02

AN Iranian newspaper is holding a contest for cartoons on the Holocaust, but so far the only submissions have been from Ted Rall, Garry Trudeau, and the **New York Times.** —Speech, CPAC, 2-10-06

CYBERCAST NEWS SERVICE: What advice would you give Tony Snow on handling the media now that he's the new White House press secretary?

COULTER: Make sure Helen Thomas passes through a metal detector.
—Interview, CNS News, 6-6-06

HANNITY: I look at somebody, though, like Bill Moyers, bitter, angry liberal. He had his whole career subsidized in part by taxpayers of this country. What does he have to be angry about?

COULTER: You dropped "paranoid megalomaniac." I don't know if you caught any of his speech last week . . . when he was reading fan letters to himself aloud and talking about how he was being persecuted by Republicans. . . . I think the next stage is germ phobia.
—*Hannity & Colmes,* 5-24-05

WE need these liberal talk-radio shows to keep the tinfoil-hat types busy while we run the country, democratize the Middle East, and secure our borders. —**Speech, Indiana University, 2-23-06**

THESE liberals, they can live Walter Mitty fantasyland lives, and the media will write down anything a liberal politician tells them. You know, [John Kerry] can start telling them, "I won the Olympic gold in swimming four years ago!" **Oh, let's get that down,** and it gets printed in the **Boston Globe.** —Interview, *New York Observer,* 9-13-04

AMERICAN journalists are upset that John Ashcroft is asking Muslims what they're doing taking flight lessons but think they can ask me about my supposed sex life. —Interview, *New York Observer,* 8-20-02

"**I CONCEDE** that at one place in the book [Ann Coulter's **Slander**] I scribbled 'good point!' in the margin (p. 108). I tell you that so you can turn to that page in the book-store and skip the painful rest." —Richard Cohen, **Washington Post,** August 15, 2002
    "I'm going to have to find out what's on page 108 and take it out!" —Ann Coulter, in e-mail, yesterday morning. —Dawson Speaks, 8-18-02

IN his speech last week [Bill Moyers] compared himself to Jesus Christ. You're really missing the total insanity of this man. . . . Having had complete hegemonic control of the entire media for forty, fifty years, and now suddenly, you know, these tiny little inroads being made by a single cable news station, talk radio, and of course, the wonderful world of the Internet—and they're having a public breakdown. I mean, look at the stream of invective at Fox News. Fox News does—and congratulations— have the top five rated talk shows on cable TV. . . . You have, what, 2 million viewers. Bill O'Reilly has 2.6 million viewers. Okay, ABC News, NBC News each have 10 million viewers apiece. Even the fake news on CBS gets 7 million viewers. So you know, this is a tiny little drop in the ocean, and suddenly, it's 1938 Germany and Bill Moyers is a Jew. —*Hannity & Colmes,* **5-24-05**

APPARENTLY, unless you call me a rotten slut, you're sucking up to me. Merely being polite and giving an honest interview to Ann Coulter, yeah, you must be sucking up. —Interview, *New York Observer,* 7-3-06

AT least the old subliminal ads for popcorn in movie theaters operated by stealth. Today's mainstream media engage in open conditioning of the public in a fantastical scheme to shift public opinion. —"Poll: Most Americans Love Coulter Columns!," 3-22-06

REPUBLICANS seem oblivious to the fact that if anyone cared what Dan Rather had to say, Republicans would not be the majority party. Republicans should be required to say this mantra over and over to themselves: "It is a good thing to be attacked by the likes of the **New York Times** and **60 Minutes,** both of which are losing readers/viewers faster than innocent bystanders exiting the Vibe Awards after another random stabbing. It is a good thing. . . ." —"It's WABBIT Season!," 11-24-04

THIS is how Bush "intimidates" the press? The level of intimidation I had in mind is more along the lines of how President

Dwight D. Eisenhower "intimidated" Julius and Ethel Rosenberg at 8 in the morning, June 19, 1953. —"*N.Y. Times:* **Better Dead Than Read**," 7-12-06

I PROMISE you, if [John] McCain, [Colin] Powell, or even Rudy Giuliani were put on the ticket, the liberal lovefest would come to a screeching halt. We'd finally get a little investigative reporting on liberals' favorite Republicans—and who knows what's in those closets. (Let's just hope McCain and Giuliani don't have any messy divorces in their past!) —"**Never Trust a Liberal Over Three**," 7-21-04

HOW, precisely, would a conservative go about eliminating liberal points of view from his life? You would have to be a survivalist in Idaho to escape the liberal sound chamber. —*Slander,* p. 116

IF Fox News were the right-wing station they claim it is, we'd have twenty-four hours of nothing but Dennis Kucinich. I'd stay home to watch that. —*Hannity & Colmes,* 1-8-04

IT'S never **Debbie Does Dallas** or the publication of classified Pentagon documents that provokes such urgent reexaminations of the First Amendment. When liberals warn that free speech imperils "the capacity of citizens to govern themselves," you know conservatives must be opening their yaps again. —*Slander,* p. 92

[C]ONSERVATIVE radio talk-show hosts have a built-in audience unavailable to liberals: people driving cars to some sort of job. —*How to Talk to a Liberal (If You Must),* p. 195

FREEDOM of speech isn't working out so well for liberals now that they aren't the only ones with a microphone. It's not so much fun when the rabbit's got the gun. —"Shock and Awe Campaign Routs Liberals," 4-10-03

RONALD REAGAN, OR WHY I SOMETIMES WAVER ON HUMAN CLONING

The idea that Reagan was some pulsively brilliant communicator is often touted, as if the core of his ability to communicate was choreography rather than morality. He was a brilliant communicator because of what he believed. Americans felt their history in him.

REAGAN'S moral crusade is smirkingly dismissed as if it amounted to nothing more than bright and sunny optimism— the equivalent of a peppy Madison Avenue jingle selling dog food. It wasn't just military might or a preference for the material- ist bounty of capitalism that drove Reagan's victory over Communism. It was Americans choosing faith in God over faith in man. —*Treason*, p. 166

Q: Liberals claimed to be horribly embarrassed by Ronald Reagan's bellicose anti-Communism. They find it impossible to recognize his role in winning the Cold War. Why?

A: They know Reagan won the Cold War; they're just annoyed with the outcome. —Interview, *Insight* magazine, 9-16-03

TO hear liberals tell it, you'd think Reagan talked about God the way Democrats do, in the stilted, uncomfortable manner of people pretending to believe something they manifestly do not. . . . Or, for that matter, the way Democrats talk about free-market capitalism. —"Let's Rewrite One for The Gipper!," 6-17-04

JUST as Watergate was payback for [Alger] Hiss, Bill Clinton was payback for Reagan. When Reagan won the Cold War, he won a fifty-year argument with liberals. —*Treason*, p. 199

NEWSWEEK's Eleanor Clift says Bush is unlike Reagan because Reagan "reached out, and he was always seeking converts." That's true, actually. I think Reagan would have favored converting Third World people to Christianity. (Now why does that idea ring a bell?) —**"Let's Rewrite One for The Gipper!,"** 6-17-04

Q: Ronald Reagan's mother's name was Nelle. Your mother's name is Nell. Nell is clearly a good, conservative person's mother's name. What's a good liberal person's mother's name?

A: Actually the ingredients are even more precise than that! To ensure a God-fearing, patriotic American, you need a mother named Nell(e) who is a Protestant and a father named Jack who is a Catholic.

As for your question—Beelzebub! —Interview, Citizenlink, 10-19-04

[**On the** New York Times's **obituary for Reagan**]
I READ the **New York Times** last week and apparently a fellow named "Iran-Contra"

died recently. But that's all I'll say about the people who have consistently been on the wrong side of history and whose publisher is a little weenie who can't read because he has "dyslexia." —"Let's Rewrite One for The Gipper!," 6-17-04

REPUBLICAN candidates ought to note that Reagan got more women to vote for him than George Bush or Bob Dole did—more than Liddy Dole did, for that matter. (Of course, Reagan also got about 40 percent more of the men's vote than did Carter.) Oh yeah, and unlike Bush Sr. and the various Doles who keep running for president, Reagan won. Twice. —"No Shadow of a Doubt—Liberal Women Are Worthless," 4-18-00

WAS Reagan "nice" to the Soviets? They certainly didn't think so. The Soviets constantly denounced Reagan as "rude," and our dear friends at the BBC upbraided Reagan for his "rude attacks" on Fidel Castro, Nicaragua, and the Soviet Union. [**Washington**] **Post** columnist [Colman] McCarthy indignantly charged that Reagan had "put down an entire nation—the Soviet Union—by calling it 'the focus of evil in the nuclear world.'"

The lesson to draw from what liberals said about Reagan then and what they are forced to say about him now is that the electable Republican is always the one liberals are calling an extremist, Armageddon-believing religious zealot.—**"Let's Rewrite One for The Gipper!," 6-17-04**

RONALD Reagan appealed to what is best about America and so transformed the nation that we are now safe to carry on without him. —**"2004: Highlights and Lowlifes," 12-29-04**

Q: [W]hat [was it] like to meet a man you admired so much, [Ronald Reagan]?

A: It was like an orthodox Jew meeting Moses.

—Interview, American Enterprise Institute, 2004

REPUBLICANS:
AREN'T THEY MAGNIFICENT?

As disappointed as many Republicans are with our presidential nominees, at least we're not running anyone named B. Hussein Obama. Or Clinton. Here is a handy summary of the leading Republican candidates' good and bad points.

Rudy Giuliani
STRENGTH: Only one of his ex-wives was in *The Vagina Monologues*.
WEAKNESS: Guns.

STRENGTH: He showed considerable leadership in New York City a few years ago. I can't remember the exact occasion, but I know it was something big . . . He was really good, though!

WEAKNESS: Gay marriage.

STRENGTH: He is a patriot—sort of like Democrats used to be when they could still get a majority of Americans to vote for them.

WEAKNESS: Little babies sleeping peacefully in their mothers' wombs.

STRENGTH: As a former prosecutor, he could lead the prosecution against Mike Nifong and other out-of-control liberal prosecutors.

John McCain

STRENGTH: Went to Vietnam.

WEAKNESS: Didn't bring a camera, like John Kerry and Al Gore.

STRENGTH: Many mainstream news outlets already believe him to be president.

WEAKNESS: About half of his policy positions.

STRENGTH: He is loved by his party (the MSM).

WEAKNESS: He is distrusted by the other party (Republicans).

Newt Gingrich

STRENGTH: People don't giggle so much anymore when they hear his name.

WEAKNESS: At this stage, he's not running.

Fred Thompson

STRENGTH: He was great in **The Hunt for Red October**!

WEAKNESS: We'll be left with only three Republicans in Hollywood (and they've asked me not to name them).

Mitt Romney

STRENGTH: As a former Massachusetts governor, he has a proven ability to trick liberals into voting for him.

WEAKNESS: Belongs to a peculiar quasi-Christian church, the Masons.

STRENGTH: He would look good on a coin or a stamp, whereas Giuliani looks like a guy in an antacid commercial.

WEAKNESS: He saved the Olympics. (I'm putting that down as a weakness because I hate the Olympics.)

STRENGTH: More cocktails for everyone else at White House dinners!

WEAKNESS: I like the torch at the beginning of the ceremonies because it contributes to global warming, but after that I'm out. I lose interest completely.

STRENGTH: No Oval Office issues, if you know what I mean.

Duncan Hunter
STRENGTH: Best man for the job.
WEAKNESS: No one knows who he is.

THE sun is brighter, the birds sing more sweetly, and men are manlier whenever a Republican is in the White House. —Interview, American Enterprise Institute, 2004

[On the 2004 Republican National Convention]
WE do this thing where the RNC goes around with a mike and sticks it in the delegate's face—they can't do that at the

Democratic Convention. Can you imagine putting a mike in a Democratic delegate's face? Who knows what they'd say? It would be, you know, "Kill the president! Long live France!" —Interview, *New York Observer*, 9-13-04

YEAR after year, Gallup polls show that more than twice as many Americans call themselves conservative (about 41 percent) than call themselves liberals (about 19 percent). The only clearly identifiable group of Americans who don't want to be identified as conservatives are Republicans in Washington. —Speech, CPAC, 2-10-06

WHY doesn't the diversity crowd ever give the Republican Party credit for placing developmentally disabled persons in a substantial majority of its leadership positions? —"Developmentally Disabled Republicans," 5-22-00

Q: Do you think a Giuliani-McCain ticket could defeat Hillary?

A:. . . If the nominees for president in 2008 are Hillary Clinton and Giuliani-McCain, who cares who wins?
—Interview, *The Jewish Press*, 3-07

FROM [Joe] McCarthy to Richard Nixon to Ronald Reagan, it is conservatives who appeal to workers. When Republicans ignite the explosive energy of the hardhats, liberals had better run for cover. —*Treason*, p. 69

Q: What do you think when you hear people argue that [Arnold] Schwarzenegger ought to represent the new face of the Republican Party?
A: I would take them more seriously if they registered as Republicans.
—Interview, American Enterprise Institute, 2004

OUR problem is exactly the reverse of the Democrats', who have to prevent the American people from understanding what they really believe. The more people know about what **we** really believe, the more they like us, as opposed to the **image** of conservative or Republican. —Interview, *New York Observer,* 1-10-05

DEMOCRATS have declared war against Republicans, and Republicans are wandering around like a bunch of ninny Neville Chamberlains, congratulating themselves on their excellent behavior. They'll have some terrific stories about their Gandhi-like passivity to share while sitting in cells at Guantánamo after Hillary is elected. —"Conservatives Need 12-Step Program to Manhood," 5-10-06

THERE are a lot of bad Republicans; there are no good Democrats. —*Lou Dobbs Tonight,* 7-21-03

WITHIN days [of the Harriet Miers nomination], every Republican in the nation was opposed to the Miers nomination, with the narrow exception of Republicans whose sole reason for being is to receive a personal phone call from Karl Rove—which wasn't bad considering that there was more dissent on a slave plantation than there is in the modern Republican Party—and you know what I'm talking about, girlfriend. (I can say that, by the way. My party freed the slaves.) —Speech, CPAC, 2-10-06

WEAK and frightened conservatives crave liberal approval and will do anything to get it. The telltale sign is how quickly a conservative will publicly attack another conservative. —*How to Talk to a Liberal (If You Must)*, p. 14

BEING a "moderate" Republican satisfies the beast only as long as they still need you for pro-abortion votes and demeaning quotes about your "fellow" Republicans. —*Slander*, p. 50

REPUBLICANS waste more time being afraid of Democrats than they do robbing orphans, evicting widows, helping corporations—you know, what we're paying them to do. —Speech, CPAC, 2-10-06

To a conservative, a scandal is when someone brazenly does something really bad, tries to conceal it, and fails; for example, what liberals have done to our public schools is a scandal. Liberals' idea of a good scandal is a highly convoluted story with lots of debatable legal points that they believe can best be explained by a meaningless, insinuating slogan. No one is ever quite sure what the scandal-plagued Republican has done, other than that, one day, he suddenly started being described as "scandal-plagued."

By contrast, anyone could plainly state a Democrat's wrongdoing in a sentence or two. For example:

- As governor of Arkansas, Bill Clinton invited a state employee, Paula Jones, to a hotel room, where he asked her to perform oral sex on him. When she sued him for sexual harassment years later, Clinton used the power of the presidency to commit a string of felonies to defeat Jones's civil rights lawsuit—including perjuring himself, tampering with witnesses, hiding evidence, and generally obstructing justice.
- Democrat House Speaker Jim Wright circumvented limits on outside income by arranging for special-interest groups to place bulk orders for his "book"—a collection of Wright's speeches—for which Wright collected an astonishing 55 percent royalty. (Come to think of it, the real scandal is the royalty percentage I'm being paid for this book.)
- Democrat Barney Frank's lover ran a homosexual prostitution ring out of Frank's Washington town house. (I know that sounds pretty innocent, but as a lawyer, I can assure you that it was illegal.)
- Democrat senator Harrison Williams, a slew of Democrat congressmen, and a

Democrat mayor (in addition to one "moderate" Republican) were nabbed in an FBI sting in 1980, accepting bribes on tape from undercover agents posing as Arab sheiks.

- Democrat president John F. Kennedy cheated on his wife with a mobster's girlfriend and mob courier.
- Democrat Wayne Hays cheated on his wife with a mistress paid for by the taxpayers.
- Democrat Gary Hart cheated on his wife while running for president. He was captured in media photos frolicking with his mistress on his lap on a boat called **Monkey Business** after daring the press to follow him.
- Democrat Chuck Robb cheated on his wife and said he was getting a back rub. As I recall, it turned out to be more of a front rub.
- Democrat Jesse Jackson cheated on his wife and had an illegitimate child while counseling Clinton on his infidelity, and used Rainbow Coalition funds to pay his mistress.

- Democrat congressman William "The Refrigerator" Jefferson was caught on videotape accepting $100,000 in bribe money. When the FBI later searched Jefferson's house, they found $90,000 in cash stuffed in his freezer.
- Democrat Sandy Berger, Bill Clinton's national security adviser, stole classified documents from the National Archives, hid them under a construction trailer, later retrieved the documents, cut them up with scissors, and threw them away. We will never know what was in those documents.

Okay, now explain "Watergate" or "Iran-Contra" in one or two sentences citing actual facts. Oh, and "Nixon shredded the Constitution!" is not the sort of fact-based explanation we're looking for.

The corpus delicti of "Iran-Contra" consisted of selling arms to Iran in its war with Iraq in order to keep two heinous regimes bleeding one another a bit longer and using the proceeds of the sales to fund anti-Communist rebels in Nicaragua. The allegedly illegal part involved the Boland Amendment, which a Democratic Congress passed specifically to prevent the Reagan administration from using U.S. funds to aid the anti-Communist Contras. (Aren't the Democrats great?) Since the money being sent to the Contras came from the Iranians and never passed through the U.S. Treasury, it did not violate any law . . . **ZZZZZZZZZZZZ** . . .

"Watergate" was an apparently pointless break-in of Democratic headquarters at the Watergate Hotel conducted by members of Nixon's campaign staff, not the White House staff. Nixon didn't know about it beforehand, much less order it, and the "cover-up" did not involve him perjuring himself, hiding evidence, or tampering with witnesses, though someone on his staff may have erased eighteen and a half minutes of a taped phone call between Nixon and his chief of staff, H. R. "Bob" Haldeman. The president merely asserted constitutional privileges to protect his allies and separate himself from the utterly common cloak-and-dagger activities of his reelection campaign staff.

Democrat scandals begin with Democrats doing something wrong. Republican scandals also begin with Democrats doing something wrong—to wit: becoming hysterical about something no one understands and then giving the alleged scandal a name, preferably ending in "gate." You will note that absurd manufactured scandals involving Republicans seem to have proliferated since 9/11. Whenever there is any external threat to the United States, the only way the Democrats can win is with another Watergate.

[**BILL CLINTON**] reminds everyone of basically the worst episode in American history: Clinton talking on the phone with congressmen about sending American troops to the Balkans while being serviced by Monica Lewinsky under the desk. And liberals didn't mind that—but they're upset that George Bush waited forty-eight hours to fly back from Crawford, Texas [after the Indonesian tsunami]. —Interview, *New York Observer,* 1-10-05

[**P**]**OLITICIANS** with something to hide—say, wild promiscuity, stupidity,

Chappaquiddick, or a former membership to the Ku Klux Klan—had best be liberals. There may be other reasons to be a liberal—generalized hatred of America, for example—but one very good reason is that you need the media's protection. Only politicians with nothing to hide dare risk displeasing the **New York Times** editorial page. —*Slander,* p. 50

FOCUSING like a laser beam on the big picture, liberals are upset that . . . the secretary of defense used an Autopen. An Autopen is a mechanical arm that actually holds a pen and is programmed to sign letters with a particular person's precise signature. Imagine a President Al Gore, with slightly more personality, signing all official government letters—that's an Autopen. (You can relax now, there will be no more exercises imagining a President Al Gore.) —"Happy Giving Tree Festival to All, and to All a Good Night!," 12-22-04

EVEN if corners were cut, [Iran-Contra] was a brilliant scheme. There is no possibility that anyone in any Democratic administration would have gone to such lengths to fund anti-Communist forces. When Democrats scheme from the White House, it's to cover up the president's affair with an intern. When Republicans scheme, it's to support embattled anti-Communist freedom fighters sold out by the Democrats. —*Treason*, p. 179

EVERY conservative public figure would need a full-time investigative and legal staff to refute the endless stream of defamatory attacks. By the time the insinuations are exposed as baseless nonsense, it's old news, yesterday's story; the media has "moved on." Meanwhile, it takes DNA evidence that the president lied under oath to get the media to take note of malfeasance by a fellow liberal. —*Slander*, p. 84

LIBERALS' comprehension of corporate scandals is like the Woody Allen joke about what he knew about **War and Peace** after taking a speed-reading course and reading it in 20 minutes: "It involves Russia." —"It's Just About Money," 7-25-02

IT is often absurdly said that scandals such as Gary Hart's affair with Donna Rice will discourage young idealists from going into politics. This is mainly said by Gary Hart. Of course, another possible response to adultery scandals involving politicians is not good people avoiding politics, but politicians avoiding adultery. —*Slander*, p. 202

TO have the president's behavior propel the country into a national discussion of whether oral sex counts as adultery would have been a black-letter "High Crime and Misdemeanor," if the framers could possibly have imagined any president would sink so low. —*High Crimes and Misdemeanors*, p. 13

WITH the Democrats' full-throated moralizing of late, I'm almost tempted to vote for them—although perhaps "full-throated" is the wrong phrase to use with regard to Democrats and sex scandals. —"Clinton's Latest Glow Job," 10-11-06

SEX: "VIRILE PACIFIST" IS AN OXYMORON

I imagine sex with a Democrat would be very complicated. They'd keep changing positions for no apparent reason and every few minutes they'd ask you if you think things were moving in the right direction. Sometimes, in the heat of passion, they'd yell out someone else's name, like "Generic Democratic Candidate!" or "Anyone But Hillary!" Republicans believe in negotiating from a position of strength. Democrats believe the first step in negotiations is to lay down their arms. Whom would you rather be ravaged by?

COLLEGE STUDENT: What do you think of premarital sex?

COULTER: Honestly, that's the worst pickup line I've ever heard.

—Interview, University of Connecticut, 12-7-05

LENO: Have you ever had sex with a liberal?

COULTER: No.

LENO: Really?

COULTER: No.

LENO: You should try it, see what it's like.

COULTER: I read about it in **Esquire**, and it does not sound good.

—*Tonight Show with Jay Leno*, 6-14-06

I DON'T share the other panelists' alarm at the idea that the federal government isn't funding "safe sex" programs. And I think it's kind of phony to say, "Well, of course we all want abstinence, but we're just going to teach them this as a backup method." It's only in the case of premarital sex by teenagers that liberals make this argument. I mean nobody says, "Well, what if a student comes to you and says I want to commit a hate crime? We want to teach them how to do it safely." —*Hardball with Chris Matthews*, 12-5-02

[**U.S.** Surgeon General C. Everett Koop] talks "about making an animated educational video that would feature two condoms 'with little eyes on them' chatting about the need for 'gentle, nonmystifying' sex education for students, starting in kindergarten." I would pay quite a bit of money to hear someone describe anal sex— oh, heck, make it any kind of sodomy— to a five-year-old in a nonmystifying way. —*Godless*, p. 180

LIBERALS seek to destroy sexual differentiation in order to destroy morality. **The Vagina Monologues** is the apotheosis of the Left's desire to treat women's sexuality like some bovine utilitarian device, stripped of any mystery or eroticism. —*Slander*, p. 28

WHEN they are young, nubile Hollywood actresses all utter the same idiotic clichés about the artistic value of nudity in movies. Then they expect us to feel sorry for them when parts dry up after they become old and start to sag. Live by the breast, die by the breast! —**"I Like Black People Too, Julia!,"** 4-1-02

SOCIETY cannot legislate what goes on "in the bedroom." But if we can't legislate what goes on in the bedroom, why can't I hide money from the IRS under my mattress? —*Godless*, p. 9

[M]OST of the [child molestation] allegations against the priests do not even constitute "sexual relations" on the Democratic Party's definition. —**"Should Gay Priests Adopt?,"** 3-21-02

THE SUPREME COURT: I HAVEN'T BEEN OFFICIALLY APPROACHED AS YET, BUT THANKS FOR ASKING

Judicial nominations during the Bush administration should have irrevocably proved:

1. Never trust Washington weenies
2. Democrats aren't that scary

During Bush's first term, a Republican lawyer for the Senate Judiciary Committee, Manuel Miranda, found memos Democrats had left in open computer files proving that the Democrats were targeting Bush's Hispanic nominees to the courts solely because they were Hispanic. Yes, the same Democrats who want us to put them in charge of national security today. Those guys.

What do you suppose the Democrats

would have done if they ever found Republican memos opposing Ruth Bader Ginsburg, say, because she was Jewish? I mean, other than the Democrats who are openly anti-Semitic, like Cynthia McKinney, Cindy Sheehan, Noam Chomsky, Jimmy Carter . . . you know, the closeted anti-Semites in the Democratic Party. The ones who haven't "come out" yet.

Miranda's discovery of these memos resulted in . . . no outrage whatsoever from the unbiased, objective mainstream media. Unless you count the outrage at Manuel Miranda himself. For reasons I still don't understand, instead of these memos being the Democrats' scandal, they became the Republicans' scandal. This was roughly the equivalent of bringing felony charges against the security guard who discovered the break-in at the Watergate Hotel in 1972 and letting everybody else walk.

The voters had a different idea.

Tom Daschle, then the Democrats' minority leader in the Senate, was the man most responsible for blocking Bush's judges in his first term. In Daschle's next election, in 2004, he lost. Senator Tom Daschle became citizen Tom Daschle—just another average guy married to a high-paid D.C. corporate lobbyist.

After the 2004 election, Republicans had an even **larger** majority in the Senate. So naturally, Republican politicians were panicked at what the Democrats might do when Bush had two seats to fill on the Supreme Court. The prospect of a U.S. Senate with one hundred Republican members was looming large.

First, the White House nominated John Roberts—Secret Service code name "Tabula Rasa"—and rushed to assure the press that Roberts had never been a member of the Federalist Society. Photos were distributed of Roberts donating to PBS, recycling aluminum cans, and tearing up while reading Maya Angelou. John Roberts is turning out to be a fine justice. But it seems pretty clear that he was put on the Supreme Court by the Bush administration completely by accident.

Next we got Harriet Miers because she had been recommended by the Democrats' new Senate minority leader, Harry Reid—a man who made Tom Daschle seem witty and charismatic. We got Harriet Miers and a plate of cookies because Washington weenies refuse to believe election results.

When conservatives complained about Miers, the Washington weenies informed us that no one else was willing to take the job—which is the runaway victor, the Triple Crown champion, the Academy Award winner of the stupidest comment ever made by a Republican. Who would want a job like Supreme Court justice? No wonder all those illegal immigrants from Mexico are willing to be Supreme Court justices for five dollars an hour! What American would take that job?

Only because of the grassroots Republican revolt against Harriet Miers were Republicans in Washington finally forced to face their worst nightmare—an out-of-the-closet conservative nominee to the Supreme Court. Or as we now call him, Justice Sam Alito.

What Washington Republicans seem not to realize is that while they fear snippy remarks from the media, Democrats fear something far more daunting to a politician: the American people. The voters. The electorate. Remember: If liberals could trust the voters, they wouldn't need the Court to invent ludicrous "constitutional rights" for them in the first place.

THE only limit on liberal insanity in this country is how many issues liberals can get before a court. —**"Place Your Right Hand on the Koran and Repeat After Me,"** 1-2-04

A LOT is at stake for liberals with the court. If they lose a liberal vote, they will be forced to fight political battles through a messy little system known as "democracy." —**"Eight More Clarence Thomases,"** 2-8-01

EVEN the wackiest Supreme Court rulings always make a big show of pretending to consult the Constitution before announcing, for example, that Christmas displays must have a particular ratio of reindeer to virgins. —**"Democrats Don't Have the Constitution for Racial Equality,"** 1-23-03

THE First Amendment has been interpreted now to protect overweight women dancing with pasties, burning the flag, but not core political speech. —*Kudlow & Company,* 7-3-06

TWO more Democrat appointments to the Supreme Court, and all sorts of speech liberals don't care for will be banned as "hate crimes" or "campaign finance" violations. But wholly nonspeech activities liberals support—including body odor and products peddled by Larry Flynt and his ilk—will be protected as "free speech." —"Courting George Orwell," 10-23-00

WHEN conservative judges strike down laws, it's because of what's in the Constitution. When liberal judges strike down laws (or impose new laws, such as tax increases), it's because of what's in the **New York Times**. —"Actually, 'Judicial Activism' Means '$E = mc^2$,'" 9-14-05

I REMEMBER a time when the word "mean" was only used by little girls. Of course, this was in a happier, gentler era— before these little girls were put on the

Supreme Court. The role of liberalism has been to elevate little girls' pouting to a societal issue. —Interview, Citizenlink, 10-19-04

SOMEDAY I'd like to see a true right-wing court just to demonstrate what "conservative" judicial activism would really look like. To correspond to the "living Constitution" wielded by liberal jurists, the court would have to start discovering constitutional clauses invalidating the income tax, prohibiting abortion across the nation, and protecting the right to suck the brains out of Democrats—all in the penumbras, you understand. —"The Supreme Court Ratchet," 9-12-00

UNFORTUNATELY for Bush, he could nominate his Scottish terrier Barney, and some conservatives would rush to defend him, claiming to be in possession of secret information convincing them that the pooch is a true conservative and listing Barney's many virtues—loyalty, courage, never jumps on the furniture . . . —"This Is What 'Advice and Consent' Means," 10-5-05

IT'S hard to say which of [Sandra Day] O'Connor's decisions was the worst. It's like asking people to name their favorite Beatle or favorite (unaborted) child. —"Reagan's Biggest Mistake Finally Retires," 7-6-05

FORTUNATELY for liberals, soccer moms hear that a [judicial] nominee is "extreme" and "out of the mainstream" and are too frightened to ask for details. (Ironically, based on ticket sales and TV ratings, soccer is also out of the mainstream.) —"The 'Mainstream' Is Located in France," 10-30-03

THE fundamental goal of the next Supreme Court justice should be to create a record that would not inspire Senator Chuck Schumer to say, as he did of Justice O'Connor last week, "We hope the president chooses someone thoughtful, mainstream, pragmatic—someone just like Sandra Day O'Connor." That's our litmus test: We will accept only judicial nominees violently opposed by Chuck Schumer. —"Reagan's Biggest Mistake Finally Retires," 7-6-05

[T]HE malleable "right to privacy" metastasized from a right to contraception for married couples to a right to destroy human life in **Roe v. Wade.** What about the poor little tyke's privacy? The question misses the point. "Constitutional right" means "Whatever Liberals Want." —*Godless,* p. 9

THE only way a Supreme Court nominee could win the approval of NARAL and Planned Parenthood would be to actually perform an abortion during his confirmation hearing, live, on camera, and preferably a partial-birth one. —**"Souter in Roberts' Clothing,"** 7-20-05

AT least [Justice Sandra Day O'Connor] would not overrule a precedent for something as trivial as a human life. Overruling a precedent would require a really, really compelling value like our right to sodomize one another. —**"Reagan's Biggest Mistake Finally Retires,"** 7-6-05

LIBERALS think they can demand a ruling from the Supreme Court that will take all risk out of trysting sex. But the High Court can't do that any more than penicillin can. Liberals seem not to realize their real complaint is with a Lawmaker whose judgment cannot be appealed. —*Godless*, p. 98

I HAVE long lobbied for Republican presidents to find eight more [Supreme Court justices] just like Clarence Thomas so we can have an all-black Supreme Court. Wouldn't that be cool? But they have to be **just** like Clarence Thomas.—**Interview,** *Il Foglio* **(Italy), 10-04**

WE need somebody to put rat poison in Justice Stevens's crème brûlée. . . . That's a joke, for you in the media. —**Q &A, Philander Smith College, 1-26-06**

I DID suggest putting rat poison in Justice Stevens's crème brûlée, and after his opinion in the **Hamdan** case last week, I think that somebody has beat me to the punch. —*Hannity & Colmes*, **7-6-06**

THE great Danish cartoon caper . . . reminds me that in the Supreme Court building there's a frieze of all of the world's lawmakers—including Muhammad. . . . So maybe we have some people who will finally take care of the Court. How about we tell the Muslims about the frieze and somebody tell Scalia, Thomas, Roberts, and Alito to stay away from work next week? **—Speech, CPAC, 2-10-06**

TAXES: HOW ABOUT AMNESTY FOR "THE WEALTHY"?

Democrats simply cannot grasp the concept of tax cuts. When President Bush was implementing his second round of tax cuts in 2003—tax cuts that applied to nearly 100 million people—liberals complained that, as the **Los Angeles Times** put it, "one group is conspicuous in its absence: several million working families whose wages are so low they qualify for 'refundable' tax credits."

In other words, there were no tax cuts for people who don't pay taxes.

The **Times** prattled on about Bush's tax plan leaving some "off the list of future tax cuts," meaning that nontaxpayers' welfare benefits would not be increased. Len Burman, codirector of the Tax Policy Center—the sort of group that gets called "independent" in the **L.A. Times**—said it was "ironic," because the people Bush's tax cuts were "excluding are the ones who basically epitomize conservative values. They're working. They're marrying. They're low-income people who are trying to get ahead." However that may be, the crucial fact leading to their exclusion from Bush's tax cut plan was: They don't pay taxes.

Failing to increase a government benefit under the Earned Income Tax Credit program is not withholding a tax cut. It's nice that they have jobs, but welfare cases aren't really relevant to a discussion of tax cuts. We'll get around to the charity cases in a moment—this is about adults who pay taxes, people who contribute to government revenues, not people who receive money from the federal government.

Why can't Democrats be honest in their language? I know liberals are constantly redefining language, but the renaming of "welfare recipients" to "taxpayers" is more than actual taxpayers should have to bear. There is more candor and integrity in a beggar. If people are going to ask me for a handout, I want them to forthrightly admit, "I am begging. Will you give me some of your money?" They don't have to grovel and crawl, but don't get mouthy with me, indignantly pretending to have been bypassed in a tax cut.

TAXES are like abortion, and not just because both are grotesque procedures supported by Democrats. You're for them or against them. —**"Put the Tax Cut in a Lock Box," 2-21-02**

LIBERALS dispute slight reductions in the marginal tax rates as if they are trying to prevent Charles Manson from slaughtering baby seals. —*Slander,* p. 2

THE "big tent" may accommodate a lot of kooks, but if the Republican Party doesn't stand for tax cuts, there's no tent: The Republican Party is just a random assemblage of people—tax-cutters, tax-gougers, whatever. —**"Abraham Jeffords," 5-31-01**

THE Democrats' solution is to raise taxes to pay for preschool child care, which will require more mothers to work outside the home to pay the taxes, which will require them to put their children in government child care. Except welfare mothers. Those are the only women in America who Democrats think should not work. —*Godless*, p. 156

THE rich are the ones who pay taxes, so of course an across-the-board tax cut helps them the most. As soon as the poor start paying their fair share of the tax burden, they'll get a tax cut too. —**"Sigh of the Crook,"** 10-6-00

THE New York Times exhorted Congress to "consider rolling back—not speeding up—the regressive parts of the president's ten-year tax." ("Regressive" means "tax cut" in **Times**-speak. "Progressive" means "Ann Pays More.") —**"Mothers Against Box Cutters Speak Out,"** 10-18-01

THE WAR ON TERRORISM: PEACENIK PACIFISTS TO THE RESCUE!

Liberals claim to be against terrorism in a theoretical sense, but they oppose any concrete action to stop it, which is kind of how I feel about adopting the metric system. All we know with any certainty is that liberals were sad the World Trade Center was destroyed. But they talk about it as if it were a cholera epidemic. How about anger? Did that emotion ever occur to any of these spineless pieces of pasta?

After the 2006 midterm elections, the new Democratic majority in Congress threatened investigations into the Bush program of listening to al Qaeda phone calls to or from America. Fortunately, Bush was able to continue monitoring al Qaeda phone calls for a few more weeks after the election, but it was mostly just calls to congratulate Nancy Pelosi.

Democrats suddenly become big civil libertarians when it comes to the government tracking terrorists in this country. If any agency of the federal government shows the slightest interest in monitoring terrorists, liberals scream that America is becoming a police state engaging in racist reprisals against innocent Muslims. **Merely having associations with terrorist groups is going to get you in trouble in Bush's Amerika!**

I notice that liberals' heightened concern with civil liberties evaporates in the case of any Duke lacrosse players falsely accused of rape. In the war on terrorism, "civil libertarian" has come exclusively to mean people who think the FBI has nothing better to do than monitor the porn websites they've recently visited.

Nor are liberals particularly concerned about the privacy of citizens who hold opposing political positions. In addition to constantly using their positions of power to pursue nonsense criminal investigations of conservatives—Tom DeLay, Rush Limbaugh, Scooter Libby—Democrats have been illegally wiretapping conservatives since long before the Patriot Act.

In **Her Way: The Hopes and Ambitions of Hillary Rodham Clinton,** authors Jeff Gerth and Don Van Natta Jr. report that Hillary personally "listened to a secretly recorded audiotape of a phone conversation of Clinton critics plotting their next attack. The tape contained discussions of another woman who might surface with allegations."

So Democrats are fine with illegal wiretaps, but only if such invasive devices are narrowly limited to use on Republicans. If a government agency is found to be listening to something as frivolous as a Muslim terrorist on Khalid Sheik Mohammed's speed dial after 9/11, liberals scream that we're living in a fascist state.

Criticize Democrats' policy positions and they will fly into a sentimental rage as if you've insulted their mothers. Then they're spoiling for a fight. They only seem to lose their nerve when their country is attacked.

Meanwhile, the conservative response to 9/11 is forthright and unambiguous: "Think therefore on revenge and cease to weep" **(Shakespeare, *Henry VI, Part 2*).**

I THINK it's unquestionable that Republicans are more likely to prevent the next attack. However, I will grant that John Kerry will improve the economy in the emergency services and body bag industry. —*Hannity & Colmes,* 9-7-04

DEMOCRATS think they have concocted a brilliant argument by saying that jihadists have been able to recruit based on the war in Iraq. Yes, I assume so. Everything the United States has done since 9/11 has galvanized the evil people of the world to fight the U.S. In World War II, some Frenchmen joined the Waffen SS, too. And the good people of the world have been galvanized to fight on the side of the U.S. The question is: Which side are the Democrats on? —"**The 'Bumper Sticker' That Blows Up,**" 7-18-07

IF liberals were half as indignant about Osama bin Laden as they are about President Bush, their objections might rate more with real Americans. —*Treason,* p. 14

[D]ESPITE the earnest pleadings of Democrats and Hollywood starlets, it turns out we actually did need to spend more money on "one more cruise missile" rather than, say, the Head Start program. —**"Mothers Against Box Cutters Speak Out,"** 10-18-01

[Y]OU'RE not a patriot in this war until a liberal has compared you to the Taliban. —**"Liberalism and Terrorism: Different Stages of Same Disease,"** 7-4-02

[T]HE [New York] **Times** is furious with Bush every single moment he delays in bringing back the halcyon days when liberals could attend Calvin Klein fashion shows free of anxiety. —**"The Eunuchs Are Whining,"** 11-1-01

THE Left's theory of a just war [has] evolved to (1) military force must never be deployed in America's self-interest, and (2) we must first receive approval from the Europeans, especially the Germans. Good thing we didn't have that rule in 1941. —**"Deploying the Marines for Gays, Feminism, and Peacekeeping," 8-22-02**

THE principal difference between fifth columnists in the Cold War versus the war on terrorism is that you could sit next to a Communist in a subway without asphyxiating. —*Treason,* p. 43

IF you are one of the millions of Americans who recently canceled your subscription to the **New York Times,** you may not know that we are in the middle of a civil liberties emergency. —**"You Don't Say," 6-19-03**

IT seems the Bush administration—being a group of sane, informed adults—has been secretly tapping Arab terrorists without warrants. —**"Why We Don't Trust You with National Security," 1-4-06**

HUMAN rights groups have responded to the capture of this major al Qaeda figure [Khalid Sheikh Mohammed] with the plea:

Don't hurt him! They are hysterical at the possibility that the government is torturing Mohammed for information. There are dark rumors that terrorists are being stripped, humiliated, strapped down, and subjected to total sleep deprivation with lights and noise. Then it turned out the hapless victims of such brutal tactics weren't terrorists, but airline passengers since Sept. 11. —"The Real Pea Is Under Democrats' Heads," 3-6-03

AMERICA abides by the Geneva Convention even in conflicts with belligerents who do not. (It comes with the territory of being the Great Satan.) —"When Johnny Comes Slinking Home," 12-13-01

A LITTLE grassy park [at the site of the World Trade Center] where people go to weep does lack something in the way of defiance. Instead of us crying, evidently many Americans feel there should be a lot of Arabs crying. —"Build Them Back," 6-6-02

SUPPOSE Bush had known nineteen Muslim immigrants planned to hijack four

planes on a certain day. What could he have done? Throw Arabs out of the country? Put them in preventive detention? Order airport security to take an extra little peek at swarthy men boarding planes? Liberals wouldn't let us do that **after** 9/11.
—*Treason,* p. 259

I'M thinking about putting up a reward on my Web page for any liberal who will mention either Afghanistan or the Kurds.
—Interview, *New York Observer,* 1-10-05

INSTEAD of wondering why foreigners hate Americans, a more fruitful inquiry for the Democrats might be to ask why Americans are beginning to hate Democrats. —*Treason,* p. 230

[W]E have to take seriously the threat that Iran has nukes. Maybe they do, maybe they don't—but they're certainly acting like they do. What if they start having one of these bipolar episodes with nuclear weapons? If you don't want to get shot by the police, don't point a gun at them—or as I think our motto should be, post-9/11:

401

Raghead talks tough, raghead faces consequences. —Speech, CPAC, 2-10-06

THERE are only two choices with savages: Fight or run. Democrats always want to run, but they dress it up in meaningless catchphrases like "diplomacy," "détente," "engagement," "multilateral engagement," "multilateral diplomacy," "containment," and "going to the UN." —**"Born to Run,"** 7-19-06

IT'S a tricky business interrogating terrorists. When questioning people who live in caves, government officials have to go pretty far just to deprive them of the comforts of home. —**"The Real Pea Is Under Democrats' Heads,"** 3-6-03

THE Democratic Party has decided to express indignation at the idea that an American citizen who happens to be a member of al Qaeda is not allowed to have a private conversation with Osama bin Laden. If they run on that in 2008, it could be the first time in history a Republican president takes even the District of Columbia.

—"Why We Don't Trust You with National Security," 1-5-06

I HAVE difficulty ginning up much interest in this story [about the National Security Agency spying on "Americans"], inasmuch as I think the government should be spying on all Arabs, engaging in torture as a televised spectator sport, dropping daisy cutters wantonly throughout the Middle East, and sending liberals to Guantánamo. But if we must engage in a national debate on half-measures: After 9/11, any president who was not spying on people calling phone numbers associated with terrorists should be impeached for being an inept commander in chief. —"Frank Rich Declares Iraq 'Box Office Poison'!," 12-21-05

CAMEL-RIDING nomads may excel at the sucker punch, but wait until they see Western civilization's response. —"Mothers Against Box Cutters Speak Out," 10-18-01

EVEN if the next attack comes tomorrow, it is worth pondering that we've gone 47 months without the savages being able to mount another terrorist attack in a country virtually designed for terrorist attacks, a country where we search the purses of little old ladies so that recent immigrants from Saudi Arabia named "Mohammed" wearing massive backpacks don't feel singled out. —**"Big Foot, Scoop Jackson Dems, and Other Myths," 8-10-05**

JOHN Kerry said of Saddam's capture, "This is a great opportunity for this president to get it right for the long term. And I hope he will be magnanimous, reach out to the UN, to allies who've stood away from us." It's as if he were reading my mind! After listening to all the bellyaching from European leftists for the past eight months, I think I speak for all Americans when I say I've been on tenterhooks waiting for the right opportunity to grovel to the French. And now we have it—a major win is the perfect opportunity! —**"It's Like Christmas in December!," 12-18-03**

IF George Bush's war on terrorism were to go as well as the Democrats' war on poverty, in a few decades we could have four times as many angry Muslims worldwide plotting terrorist violence against Americans. —"No Quagmire Here!," 9-4-03

AFTER another terrorist attack, I'm sure a **New York Times** reporter could explain to the victims' families that, after all, the killer's ties to al Qaeda were merely "dubious" and the FISA court had a very good reason for denying the warrant request. —"Why We Don't Trust You with National Security," 1-5-06

Democratic strategist **RICHARD ABORN:** The Republicans refuse to discuss these issues. There is no way with any sort of credibility . . .

COULTER: I'm discussing it. You're whining. I'm discussing. We fight back. We are for preemptive attacks. You guys aren't. You want to try them in court. We want to treat it like a war. There are differences between the parties. You people scream that John Ashcroft has imposed, you know, fascism in America like he's chasing Muslims around with a stick. It's about which side is going to fight terrorism with greater force. And I'm talking about the issues, and you're saying, "Oh, boo hoo hoo, that's mean." —*Hannity & Colmes*, 9-7-04

AMERICA'S war with Islamic fanaticism didn't start on 9/11, but it's going to end with 9/11—as long as Americans aren't foolish enough ever to put a Democrat in the White House. —**"More of Kerry's Retroactive Campaign Promises,"** 7-26-06

THE greatest threat to the war on terrorism isn't the Islamic insurgency—our military can handle the savages. It's traitorous liberals trying to lose the war at home. And the greatest threat at home isn't traitorous liberals—it's patriotic Americans, also known as "Republicans," tut-tutting the quaint idea that we should take treason seriously. —**"12 Down: Top Secret War Plans, 36 Across: Treason,"** 6-27-06

[**AL**] Gore said foreigners are not worried about "what the terrorist networks are going to do, but about what we're going to do." Good. They should be worried. They hate us? We hate them. Americans don't want to make Islamic fanatics love us. We want to make them die. —*Treason,* p. 230

FOR reasons I cannot understand, I am often asked if I still think we should invade their countries, kill their leaders, and convert them to Christianity. The answer is: Now more than ever! —*How to Talk to a Liberal (If You Must),* p. 19

FINALLY, a word to those of you out there who have yet to be offended by something I have written or said: Please be patient. I am working as fast as I can.
—*"Godless* Causes Liberals to Pray . . . for a Book Burning," 6-21-06

ACKNOWLEDGMENTS

To help liberals with their blacklisting, I shall provide a list of names of the people who helped me with this book in alphabetical order. Also, I wish to thank the members of the Ann Coulter chatroom, who were enlisted to provide their favorite Ann Coulter quotes by the moderator, Brian Sullivan, and liberal-hate websites, which have been meticulously maintaining my best quotes for years (some of which I actually said!). As usual, great big heaping thanks to the brilliant comedy writer Ned Rice.

Bill Armistead
Steve Bujno
Hans Bader
Trish Baker

Jon Caldara
Robert Caplain
Mallory and Thomas Danaher
Steve Gilbert
Melanie Graham
James Higgins
Jim Hughes
Mark Kielb
Jon Ledecky
David Limbaugh
Jay Mann (who also helped with **Godless,**
    as noted in the updated acknowledg-
    ments in the paperback)
Gene Meyer
Jim Moody
Ned Rice
Ned Rice
Ned Rice
Dan Travers
Jon Tukel
Jimmie "JJ" Walker
Bill Zachary

Special thanks to the man without whom most of you would not know my name, my long-term publisher, Steve Ross. After publishing my last four massive bestsellers—when no one else would—and seeing through much of this book, including choosing the title, Steve has moved to another (very lucky) publishing house, which shall go unnamed but is the one that killed **Slander.** So they need him!

Thanks to my fabulous editor, Jed Donahue, my new publisher, Tina Constable—the only person who could possibly fill Steve's shoes—and my tremendous agents, Mel Berger and Suzanne Gluck. And of course my agent for life, Joni Evans.

I also wish to thank Lisa DePasquale, who reviewed tapes, Nexis transcripts, eight years of columns, five books, and random interviews to gather the bulk of the quotes used in this book. Lisa is now America's leading Ann Coulter historian.

In anticipation of a rollicking book tour, I thank my official book publicist, Diana Banister, and my unofficial publicist and No. 1 Ann Coulter fan, my mother, who also helped pick quotes, but was somewhat overinclusive, picking every sentence I've ever uttered.

ABOUT THE AUTHOR

ANN COULTER is the #1 **New York Times** bestselling author of **Godless, How to Talk to a Liberal (If You Must), Treason, Slander,** and **High Crimes and Misdemeanors.** She is the legal correspondent for **Human Events** and a syndicated columnist for Universal Press Syndicate. You can read her weekly column on her website, **www.anncoulter.com.**

LIKE WHAT YOU'VE SEEN?

If you enjoyed this large print edition of
**IF DEMOCRATS HAD ANY BRAINS,
THEY'D BE REPUBLICANS,** here is another book
by Ann Coulter also available in large print.

GODLESS
(hardcover)
978-0-7393-2633-6 • 0-7393-2633-3
$30.95/$41.95C

Large print books are available wherever books
are sold and at many local libraries.

All prices are subject to change. Check with your
local retailer for current pricing and availability.
For more information on these and other large print titles,
visit www.randomhouse.com/largeprint